How to Study the Bible Pt. 2

Systematic Theology

BRYAN MEADOWS

How to Study the Bible: Part 2
Systematic Theology
Bryan Meadows

©2021, Bryan Meadows
www.bryanmeadows.com
bryan@embassychurchatl.com

Published by Embassy Advantage™

Cover Design by Jason Long

Editing Team:
Tiffany Buckner
Vanessa Hunter
Georgie-Ann Neil
Nicole McCray

Research Team:
Tiffany Buckner
Vanessa Hunter
Georgie-Ann Neil
Nicole McCray
Glenda Giles

ISBN: 978-1-7348612-5-9

This book contains material protected under International and Federal Copyright Laws and Treaties. Any unauthorized reprint or use of this material is prohibited. No part of this book may be reproduced or transmitted in any form or by any means, electronic or mechanical, including photocopying, recording, or by any information storage and retrieval system without express written permission from the author/publisher.

Although the author and publisher have made every effort to ensure that the information in this book was correct at press time, the author and publisher do not assume and hereby disclaim any liability to any party for any loss, damage, or disruption caused by errors or omissions, whether such errors or omissions result from negligence, accident, or any other cause.

Unless otherwise noted, Scripture quotations are taken from The Holy Bible, New King James Version® (NKJV). Copyright© 1982 by Thomas Nelson. Used by permission. All rights reserved.

Scriptures taken from the NEW AMERICAN STANDARD BIBLE®,
Copyright©1960,1962,1963,1968,1971,1972,1973,1975,1977,1995 by The Lockman

Foundation. Used by permission.

Scripture quotations marked NIV are taken from The Holy Bible, New International Version ®, NIV ®, Copyright 1973, 1978, 1984, 2001 by Biblica, Inc.™ Used by permission. All rights reserved.

Scriptures marked AMP are taken from the AMPLIFIED BIBLE (AMP): Scripture taken from the AMPLIFIED® BIBLE, Copyright © 1954, 1958, 1962, 1964, 1965, 1987 by the Lockman Foundation Used by Permission. (www.Lockman.org)

Scripture quotations marked NLT are taken from The Holy Bible, New Living Translation, Copyright© 1996. Used by permission of Tyndale House Publishers, Inc., Wheaton, Illinois 60189. All rights reserved.

Scripture quotations marked MSG, or The Message are taken from The Holy Bible, The Message. Copyright© 1993, 1994, 1995, 1996, 2000, 2001, 2002 by NavPress Publishing Group. Used by permission. All rights reserved.

Scripture quotations marked ESV are taken from The Holy Bible, English Standard Version®. English Standard Version are registered trademarks of Crossway®.

Table of Contents

Getting Started VII
    How to Use this Guide VII
    Common Mistakes VIII

How to Study the Bible 1
    Styles of Study 6
        The Sprinkle Maneuver 6
        The Immersion Maneuver 7
        The Submersion Maneuver 7

Read the Bible in One Year 9

Studying the Bible 9
    The SOAP Method 10
    The "Other" SOAP Method 10
    My SOAP Method 11
    Hermeneutics (Recap) 12
    Extracting Knowledge, Understanding, Wisdom 13
    Why Should We Study the Word? 19
    Bible Journaling 21
    Alphabetize Your Study Time 23

List of Bible Symbols 27

Bible Book Abbreviations 30

The Foundations of Faith 33
    The Sizes of Faith 36
    The Pulse of Faith 38
    Pillars of Faith (Synonyms) 39
    Abraham, the Father of Faith 40
    The Faith of Abraham 42
    Faith Scriptures 47

The Face of God 48

From Salvation to Eschatology 50
    Damnation 51
    The Sentence 54
    The First and the Second Death 56
    More Facts About Biblical Deaths 57
    The Creation of Mankind 58
    The Death of Man, the Emergence of Mankind 59

Understanding Eschatology 63
    Premillennialism 64
    Postmillennialism 65

    Amillennialism..65
   Four Approaches to Eschatology...66
   Hell, Hades, Sheol, Gehenna, the Abyss and the Lake of Fire..67
   Gehenna and the Abyss...69
   Lake of Fire..72
   Understanding Soteriology..75
   Scriptures About Salvation..78
   Understanding Christology..82
   Trinitarianism vs. Unitarianism..82

The Spirit World...84
   Spiritual Mediators..84
   Angelogy vs. Demonology..85
   The Creation of Angels...89
   Types of Angels..90
   Facts About Angels...91
   The Great Angelic Fall..91
   The Kingdom of Darkness..92
   The Kingdom of God...93
   Types of Demons..95
   Facts About Demons..96
   Demon Stories in the Bible...97

False Doctrine and Biblical Misinterpretation..102
   Rebellion Against God..103
   The Mixing of What is Sacred with What is Profane...104
   Ungodly Relationships..105
   Religious Feuds..106
   Over-Emphasis on a Set of Scriptures...107
   Biblical Misinterpretation...109

How to Judge Prophecy...111
   Judging Prophets..113
   Measuring Fruits...114
   Judging Prophecies..116
   Other Prophetic Facts to Consider...117
   Gifts of the Spirit...118
   Scriptures About False Prophets..119
   Major and Minor Prophets in the Bible...121

Identification of and Deliverance from Cults...123
   Going Inside the Mind of a Cult Leader..124
   50 Characteristics of a Cult...128
   Cult Facts..133
   Deliverance from Cults...134

Understanding the Occult and Pagan Practices **136**
The Genesis of Occult Practices 136
The Origin of Witchcraft 139
The Revelation of Occult Practices 141
Rebellion is As the Sin of Witchcraft 143
Facts About the Tower of Babel 146
The Way, the Truth, and the Life 146
List of Common Pagan Practices 150
12 Reasons People Turn to the Occult (Witchcraft) 150
Scriptures About Witchcraft 151

12 Tribes of Israel **154**
The Gifts of God **154**
Bible Facts **156**
More Bible Facts 157

Apostasy, Heresy, Blasphemy **159**
Seven Churches in Revelations **162**
Test Your Knowledge **166**
Books of the Bible (Exam) 167
Bible Facts (Activity) 168
Questions and Answers 169
Bible Symbols (Exam) 172
Seven Churches (Exam) 173

GETTING STARTED

Welcome to a renewed way of viewing and studying the Bible. Here's a fact to get started with: you can only apply what you understand. Anything outside of the realm of understanding is called chance; in other words, what you're essentially doing is gambling with the Word. You're tossing it like a pair of dice, hoping that you'll get lucky, and this mode of study and application creates doubt, religiousness, and a works mentality. This is why I created *How to Study the Bible*! My objective is to help you find the style of biblical study and application that works best for you.

Over the course of time, people have attempted to study the Bible using the same format of reading and comprehension that was taught to them in school. The problem with this is—not everyone learns the same way. Additionally, our educational system taught us to memorize but not necessarily understand words, numbers, and facts. So, we can readily identify the words on a page, but most of us don't have full comprehension of what we're reading. This is why it's so easy for us to read one verse in the Bible and completely forget what we've just read in a matter of minutes! The Bible tells us to meditate on the Word of God. What this means is that God wants us to take His Word into our minds, and then transfer it into our hearts through a series of study, meditation, and prayer. He also wants us to attend our local assemblies so that we can get a greater understanding of not only what He said but why He said it. Without the "why," understanding is impossible to attain.

How to Study the Bible is a book designed to aid you in the study and application of the Word of God. In this guide, I've extracted many biblical facts from the Bible and other resources, and I've compiled them here so that you can take the information and revelation from the pages and transfer them to your memory bank. From there, you can withdraw and apply that information whenever you need to.

How to Use this Guide

This book is filled with biblical facts that have been extracted for you to study. To get started, make sure that you have your Bible ready and an apparatus like a pen, notepad, phone, or computer in front of you. Also, you will need:
1. To find a quiet space in your home or wherever you plan to study. Make sure you're not distracted by anything or anyone.
2. Choose the best time of day to start your Bible study. For many people, the best time to study is when the members of their households are asleep.
3. Create a welcoming atmosphere in your home or place of study. Note: one of the

reasons some people find it hard to study the Bible is because they attempt to do so in chaotic environments. They are either surrounded by junk, bills, pictures, or something that keeps serving as a distraction. This is why many people in the older generation literally had prayer closets. They used this space to pray and to study so that they could escape all the things and the people that would covet their attention.

4. Use a fresh notebook or create a new document on your phone or computer to take notes; this is so that you don't have trouble locating these notes whenever you sit down to study.
5. Write down anything that you have trouble memorizing or anything that stands out to you and study it. Utilize Google (or whatever search engine you prefer), along with your Bible.
6. Every time you sit down to read more of this book, be sure to go over what you learned the day prior.
7. Test your knowledge! Use the worksheets at the back of this book to test your knowledge! Test your knowledge after reading a chapter and take that same test the next day to ensure that you've remembered what you learned the day prior. Be sure to test yourself once a week on everything you've learned that week.
8. Apply what you've learned! Application takes the information and marries it to your belief system. In other words, it helps you to remember what you've learned.

Common Mistakes

As in all things, there is a wrong way and a right way to study the Bible. Below, you'll find a few mistakes that people commonly make.

1. **Studying with the wrong motive!** If your goal is to learn the Word so that you can appear to be smart, you will find it difficult to commit to a regular study schedule. All the same, you'll gather knowledge, but no understanding, which is the very backdrop of religion. Second Timothy 2:15 says it this way, "Study to shew thyself approved unto God, a workman that needeth not to be ashamed, rightly dividing the word of truth." Why should I study? To show myself approved! Am I trying to get approved for Heaven? No. What then am I applying for? The answer is, I'm studying so that I can withdraw whatever it is that I need from Heaven whenever I need it. In order for God to approve this withdrawal, He has to see faith. And, of course, according to Romans 10:17, faith comes by hearing and hearing by the Word of God. In other words, I must know what the Word says, apply what the Word says (faith without works is dead), and believe what the Word says. And my motive must be to glorify God, not myself!
2. **Studying at the wrong time.** We have synced our bodies and our minds to our environments, atmospheres, and schedules. And now, we have to incorporate true Bible

study (not just Bible reading) into our daily schedules. To do this, we have to find the time that works best for us individually. For example, early in the morning is a great time to study the Bible, BUT if you have a habit of getting up late and rushing to get to work, it goes without saying that mornings are not the best time for you to study. This is because if you attempt to study the Word in the morning, you will read the scriptures instead of studying the Word (the person of Jesus Christ). So maybe the best time for you to study is on your lunch break or at home before you go to bed. Then again, some people study their Bibles outside their homes (while in their cars), normally after they've returned home from work. They literally pull into their driveways and start studying! Again, you have to find what works best for you!

3. **Having no study plan.** It is always a great idea to know what, where, and when to study. One way of doing this is to start where you left off or study a specific subject like tithing, fear, or faith. If you are going to study this way, you'd have to search online for scriptures on whatever it is that you're studying.

4. **Being inconsistent.** Inconsistency disallows you from creating a habit of reading the Bible. This allows you to be led by your emotions and your personal schedule, thus, causing you to subject God to your timing and feelings, and not the other way around. Create a schedule and study the Bible consistently every day at that time. It typically takes 17-21 days to establish a habit, so this is something you want to do daily until it becomes a must-do or a habit for you.

5. **Studying when you're tired!** The average American likes to wind down before reading/studying the Bible! This can be good for some, but for most people, it doesn't necessarily work well because your mind will want to do what your body is doing—it will want to relax! Sure, go somewhere and get comfortable, but don't wait until you've poured yourself out all day long, taken your shower and climbed into bed before reading the Bible. Study when your mind is fully alert and ready to learn! Note: We often overindulge in the information we find on social media when, in truth, whenever we find ourselves tempted to go on social media, we should (instead) open our Bibles and study. After we're done, we can give what's left of our attention to social media.

6. **Mystifying the Bible.** A lot of believers have no arranged order in which they study the Bible, so consequently, they flip through the pages and read the page that opens up for them. They believe that by doing this, they are prophetically reading what God wants them to read, not realizing that this is okay sometimes, but it is NOT the way to study the Word. The mystification of God has caused many believers to search out the mysteries of God without having a revelation of God through His Word. What this means is that they want the deep things, but not the foundation. This mode of "study" only leads believers to become more mystical, emotional, and impractical in their application of the Word.

How to Study the Bible

If we can be honest, our educational system has failed us. We were taught to memorize everything; we weren't taught to understand what we were committing to memory. When learning the alphabet, we were taught the Alphabet song, and while it was relatively effective, it did little to help us in the area of comprehension. Of course, we can't put the full weight on the educational system, given the fact that our parents were supposed to do their part in ensuring that we understood what we were learning. Instead, many of our parents were caught up in the American job market; they rarely had enough time to teach us. Consequently, America (and many other Western nations) is filled with people who "know" a lot but don't necessarily "understand" what they know. This is why we are so opinionated, religious, and addicted to conspiracy theories. And believe it or not, this system of thinking has crossed over into our Bible study efforts. Ask the average American how long he or she can sit still and read the Bible, and you'll find that most believers can only seem to commit to 15 minutes (or less) of Bible study time. All the same, there is a loud cry in America that can be heard by every religion, and that is the infamous cry of "church hurt." Of course, this hurt is primarily associated with Christian faiths, especially charismatic Christianity. And while we can never invalidate, discount or discredit the experiences of another human being, I think it's safe to say that a large amount of "church hurt" is the direct result of Christians putting the full weight and responsibility of their faith on their pastors. What does this mean? It means that many believers don't have a personal, intimate, consistent and tangible relationship with the Lord. They rely solely on their leaders to tell them what "thus sayeth the Lord," and this has opened the door for many false prophets, false teachers, and immature leaders to arise. The truth is that the American church is under attack, and we have ourselves to blame for it. To counter this attack, we must get knowledge, understanding, and most of all, wisdom. And in order for this to happen, we must study the Bible. The million-dollar question is, "How should I study the Bible?" First and foremost, you must remember these facts:

1. The goal is NOT to memorize scriptures so that you can effectively quote them.
2. The goal is NOT to read the entire Bible as fast as you can (even though I completely support believers reading the Bible in a year just so that they can see that it is possible to do so).
3. The goal **is** to know Jesus all the more.

If you can remember your objective, that is to build a relationship with the Most High God, studying the Bible will become less taxing, mundane, and rhythmic. Instead, you will love coming to know the Creator because your study time will be more about building, enhancing, and developing your relationship with Him. But this requires you to utilize a system of learning that you may not be too familiar with, and that is systematic learning or, better yet, systematic theology when learning about YAHWEH. But what exactly is systematic theology? The following definition was taken from Wikipedia, and it sums it up well.

Systematic Theology
Systematic theology is a discipline of Christian theology that formulates an orderly, rational, and coherent account of the doctrines of the Christian faith. It addresses issues such as what the Bible teaches about certain topics or what is true about God and his universe. It also builds on biblical disciplines, church history, as well as biblical and historical theology. Systematic theology shares its systematic tasks with other disciplines such as constructive theology, dogmatics, ethics, apologetics, and philosophy of religion.
Source: Wikipedia

In short, systematic theology is the methodological approach of organizing the scriptures or basically creating a system that allows you to take a particular doctrine and research all there is to say about that doctrine. It then seeks to formulate a theme or a thematic approach to understanding each doctrine. Systematic theology houses ten basic categories, which are:

1. **Anthropology (Theological):** The study of humanity.
2. **Angelogy:** The study/examination of angels.
3. **Biblical Theology:** The study of the Bible and its doctrines.
4. **Christology:** The study/examination of Christ's life and purpose.
5. **Ecclesiology:** The study of the Church and the origins of Christianity.
6. **Eschatology:** The study of the end times and the final destination of the human soul.
7. **Hamartiology:** The study of sin and its effects.
8. **Pneumatology:** The study/examination of the Holy Spirit.
9. **Soteriology:** The study of salvation (through Jesus Christ).
10. **Theology (Proper):** The study and examination of God's character.

Systematic theology answers the question, "What does the Bible have to say about a specific topic?" It means to search the Bible for every scripture relating to that subject, and then to categorize those scriptures. The goal is to understand what God has to say regarding that subject. For example, let us say that you want to study the subject of faith. In simplistic terms, you'd find every scripture relating to faith. The ultimate goal is to not only know what God has to say, but to understand what He said; this way, we can enhance our relationship with Him and become more effective witnesses for Christ. All the same, this helps to secure us so that we are not "tossed to and fro by every wind of doctrine" (see Ephesians 4:4).

How then can you apply systematic theology to your study time?
1. Pray before you get started.

2. Find out what God is saying in that hour. For example, what has been your dominant thought today? Study scriptures relating to it!
3. Once you've determined your subject matter, research it. Thankfully, we no longer have to go to the public library and search through encyclopedias, thesauruses, or dictionaries to get information. Simply use the search engine of your choice; for example, conduct a search for scriptures about faith.
4. Write down what you find. Record the scriptures relating to the subject matter; be sure to highlight those scriptures in your Bible.
5. Study each scripture thoroughly and note how they relate to other scriptural passages.

Always remember to take notes and make sure that those notes are neat and well organized. Refer to those notes as much as humanly possible. Again, the goal isn't just to commit what you're studying to memory; the goal is for you to understand what you've studied. And hear me—the revelation of God is unsearchable, meaning you'll never have all you need to know regarding a specific subject! You can always go deeper! There's nothing wrong with being "deep," the problem occurs when people go deep into knowledge, but they somehow miss understanding. This causes them to lean to their own understanding, which according to Proverbs 3:5, is error! In this book, you will learn how to go into the depths of knowledge and bring out understanding. And within the depths of understanding, you will find the wisdom of God!

Books of the Bible

Use this chart to memorize the books of the Bible.
On the next page, you will find a color chart associated with each alphabet to aid you in remembering the books.

Genesis	Exodus	Leviticus	Numbers	Deuteronomy	Joshua
Judges	Ruth	1 Samuel	2 Samuel	1 Kings	2 Kings
1 Chronicles	2 Chronicles	Ezra	Nehemiah	Esther	Job
Psalms	Proverbs	Ecclesiastes	Solomon	Isaiah	Jeremiah
Lamentations	Ezekiel	Daniel	Hosea	Joel	Amos
Obadiah	Jonah	Micah	Nahum	Habakkuk	Zephaniah
Haggai	Zechariah	Malachi	Matthew	Mark	Luke
John	Acts	Romans	1 Corinthians	2 Corinthians	Galatians
Ephesians	Philippians	Colossians	1 Thessalonians	2 Thessalonians	1 Timothy
2 Timothy	Titus	Philemon	Hebrews	James	1 Peter
2 Peter	1 John	2 John	3 John	Jude	Revelation

Alphabet Color Chart

A	Amos, Acts
B	
C	1 Chronicles, 2 Chronicles, 1 Corinthians, 2 Corinthians, Colossians
D	Deuteronomy, Daniel
E	Exodus, Ezra, Esther, Ecclesiastes, Ezekiel, Ephesians
F	
G	Genesis, Galatians
H	Hosea, Habbakuk, Haggai, Hebrews
I	Isaiah
J	Joshua, Judges, Job, Jeremiah, Joel, Jonah, John, James, 1 John, 2 John, 3 John, Jude
K	1 Kings, 2 Kings
L	Leviticus, Lamentations, Luke
M	Micah, Malachi, Matthew, Mark
N	Numbers, Nehemiah, Nahum
O	Obadiah
P	Psalms, Proverbs, Philippians, Philemon, 1 Peter, 2 Peter
Q	
R	Ruth, Romans, Revelation
S	1 Samuel, 2 Samuel, Solomon
T	1 Thessalonians, 2 Thessalonians, 1 Timothy, 2 Timothy, Titus
U	
V	
W	
X	
Y	
Z	Zephaniah, Zechariah

Styles of Study

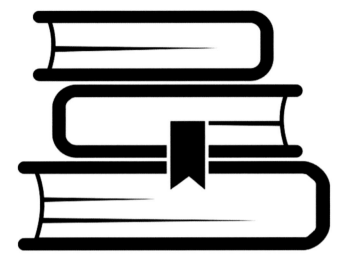

The styles of study listed below are refreshers from *How to Study the Bible* (Part One).

There are many styles of studying the Bible, but below, I'll detail three main styles, all of which I've named to help you memorize your particular style. Try them all to see what works best for you.

The Sprinkle Maneuver

This approach is for believers who are easily distracted and find it hard to study the Word in one setting. Before I detail the steps to studying the Bible using this method, let me say this—you can graduate from one style of study to another. If you're young in the faith, chances are, you may have to start with the Sprinkle Maneuver, but the goal is for you to gain control over your mind so that you can eventually become attracted to the Word and learn to study the Word more thoroughly, intentionally and intensively.

To apply the Sprinkle maneuver, follow these steps:
1. Choose what book and chapter of the Bible you plan to study throughout the day on every given day.
2. Look to see how many verses are in that chapter and divide that number by four. The reason you need to do this is because you're going to stretch your Bible study time out over the course of four hours. So, for example, if you're reading John 1, which has 50 verses, you'd divide 50 by four. The answer is 12.5, so you'd read 12 verses every hour or every other hour and 14 verses in your last setting. And don't just read each scripture, study and meditate on the Word. Reading engages your reading comprehension, as taught to you in school. This can prove to be relatively ineffective when studying the Bible. Instead, study each scripture by (1) repeating it several times, and (2) studying the

key words within each verse. At the end of the day, read the book of your choice in its entirety. This is to refresh your memory and to stabilize your attention span.

The Immersion Maneuver

This is the study style that most believers practice and hear me—if this style does not work for you, do NOT feel pressured to adopt it as your own. Over time, you will find the study style that best suits you!

Immersion is as it sounds. Think of a bath. When a person is placed in a bathtub or sits in a bathtub, that person's head is above the water; this is called immersion. Please note that the head represents authority. In this style of study, what you're basically doing is reading a book of the Bible in its entirety but running each verse of scripture through your mind until you either remember the verse in its entirety or you remember some of the key words in the verse. What you'll also need to do is study those key words or any words that stick out to you. Also, engage your mind by activating each verse. For example, let's look at John 14, which reads, "The Word became flesh and made his dwelling among us. We have seen his glory, the glory of the one and only Son, who came from the Father, full of grace and truth."

The Word (keyword) became flesh (keyword) and made His dwelling among us. To better understand this, I would first study scriptures about the Word, for example, John 1:1, Revelation 19:3, and Hebrews 4:12. Next, I'd move on to flesh, and I'd start with the making of the first Adam (Genesis 2:7). I'd then study the works of the flesh (Galatians 5:19-21). What I am able to extract from this so far is that the Word (Jesus) stepped into the sin nature of a human and overcame the flesh; that is, the temptations. This would lead me to Hebrews 2:18, which reads, "For since He Himself was tempted in that which He has suffered, He is able to come to the aid of those who are tempted."

The Submersion Maneuver

When someone is submerged in water, that person's entire body, including his or her head, is under the water. The person is hidden, and only the water can be seen. This is when you bathe or, better yet, drown yourself in the Word! Using this style of learning, you'd create a rigorous study schedule where you'd read the Bible two to three times a day (at minimum) for a period of one or more hours. You'd use sticky notes to post up scriptures all around your house so that everywhere you look, you will see the Word of God. And of course, people who use this method post up scriptures in their workplaces, in their cars, and just about every place they frequent.

This approach is designed to submerge the student in scriptures, thus, forcing the student to see and study the Word, even when he or she goes, for example, to the refrigerator or to the bathroom. This is effective when you post up notes in the rooms that you frequent the most. Some people even go to sleep with a Bible app playing on their phones so that they can subliminally implant the scriptures into their memories. And of course, some believers would say that this method is "too extreme," but that is just their opinion. Not everyone is a student of the Word; some people are visitors, meaning they visit the scriptures, but they don't necessarily take them in their hearts with them. If you are a student, you need to immerse or submerge yourself in the Word of God.

"Study to shew thyself approved unto God, a workman that needeth not to be ashamed, rightly dividing the word of truth."
2 Timothy 2:15

Read the Bible in One Year

It should be the goal of every believer to read the Bible from cover to cover several times over the course of this event we call life. But how can this be achieved? It's simple math.
- There are 365 days in a year.
- Divide the number of pages in your Bible by 365 and read that number of pages a day for a year.

For example, if your Bible has 1,281 pages, you would, divide 1281 by 365. This would come out to 3.5, which would mean your goal should be to read around four pages a day everyday for a year. Also, if you read three chapters of the Bible every day and five chapters on Sundays, you will complete Bible in one year.

Studying the Bible

Keep in mind that reading the Bible is not the same as studying the Word. The Bible is the book that contains the Logos Word, but Jesus is the Living Word of God. What this means is that reading does not equate to relationship! Some people read the Bible just so they can argue with Christians, but your primary goal for reading the Bible should be to study the heart and movements of the Most High God. The goal is to build a relationship with Him by aligning yourself with His Word. But how does one study the Bible? Here are a few tips:

1. Before studying every day, make sure that you have your Bible (obviously), a notebook (printed or digital), and a writing device. Also, if you are using a printed Bible (recommended), make sure that you have a highlighter nearby.
2. Go into a quiet room so that you're not easily distracted. (Note: if you are a parent, you may have to wait until the children are fast asleep.)
3. Start wherever you want to start or wherever the Holy Spirit leads you. (Note: don't be a super-spiritual Bible flipper with no study regime. In other words, don't just flip through the pages of the Bible, reasoning within yourself that wherever the book opens, that's where God wants you to read. Find a spot and start your reading.)
4. Highlight the text that speaks to you the most and be sure to define the words that you don't fully understand. You can compare the version of the Bible that you're reading with other translations by simply reading other translations online.
5. Meditate on the Word! Rehearse some of the scriptures in your mind time and time again. Write those scriptures on sticky notes and post them throughout your home. This will help you to retain what you've read.

You can also:
1. Study the action words (verbs) in each verse.
For example, "God so loved the world" or "Bring ye all the tithes..." Be sure to use a Concordance as well!

2. Create an outline.
Write down the main subjects and then write down a list of questions. Be sure to do your research and answer those questions. For example:

Text	Thou shalt love thy neighbor as thyself
Questions	What is a neighbor? What are the Greek and Hebrew words for neighbor? What is love?

3. Phone a friend.
Having a study partner helps to keep you from rushing through study time and allows you to get the most out of what you're reading.

The SOAP Method

Scripture	Observation	Application	Prayer

Scripture
Write down a scripture.

Observation
What stands out in the scripture that you're reading? What words are being used repetitiously?

Application
How can you apply what you've read to your life? In this, you make the scripture personal.

Prayer
Pray about what you've read and what you've extracted from it.

The "Other" SOAP Method

The SOAP method is used by healthcare providers, but can be very effective when studying

Studying the Bible

the Word as well. Use this method, for example, when you are studying something specific. Let's say that you were dealing with mental warfare brought on by rejection. You could use this method to study rejection; this way, you can effectively defeat it.

| Subjective | Objective | Assessment | Plan |

Subjective
Document the signs, symptoms, and problems that are present in your life.

Objective
The objective should include everything you can measure, for example, a decline in energy, inability to worship, trouble getting out of bed.

Assessment
Here, you document your thoughts about the issue; for example, what triggered you to feel the way that you feel. or you can ask yourself, "Is this a recurring issue?"
If so, what event typically triggers those emotions.

Plan
If you decide, for example, that you're wrestling with rejection, you'd do research using your Concordance and your favorite search engine on rejection. You'd then list the scriptures that come up, study those scriptures and develop a plan to combat rejection using those scriptures.

My SOAP Method

| Scripture | Organize | Assemble | Preach |

Scripture
Write down the scriptures that you want to study.

Organize
Create a few categories and list the words that stick out under one of those categories.
"For God so loved the world, that he gave his only begotten Son, that whosoever believeth in him should not perish, but have everlasting life."

Action (Verbs)	Loved	Gave
Believe	Should Not Perish	Have (Possess)

Assemble

Pair those words up with other words that are relative to them. For example, one of the action words is "loved." So, I'd list scriptures about love like, "God is love" and "But God demonstrates his own love for us in this: While we were still sinners, Christ died for us."

Preach

Note: you don't need a platform to do this. You simply need to take what you've learned and encourage yourself with it. Also, whenever you talk to your friends or loved ones, talk about what you've learned. This will help you retain the information so that you can effectively and consistently apply it to your life!

Hermeneutics (Recap)

Let's revisit the hermeneutics chart from How to Study the Bible (Part One).

Literal Interpretation	Moral Interpretation	Allegorical Interpretation
This approach takes the biblical text word-for-word, giving no room for prophetical utterances, parables or any other translations. A lot of the biblical text is literal, but some of it is allegorical or metaphorical. The Bible was not written for mankind to "understand". It was literally written for the believer; its many mysteries can only be understood by Spirit-filled believers to whom understanding has been granted!	This approach deals primarily with ethics. The goal here is to read between the lines to extrapolate the moral lesson behind each story or scripture, and how to apply what was extracted to our everyday lives.	This approach deals more with symbolism. For example, the Church is allegorically understood to be the Bride of Christ, Jerusalem is used to allegorically represent Heaven, etc. The allegorical approach is designed to take what people understand (natural things) and use it as a reference point to help them better understand spiritual things.

Reminder: None of these approaches are wrong; this is why you have to be led by the Spirit of God, and not allow pride to tempt you into giving an answer when you don't have a foundation for that answer. As you venture further into this guide, you will see examples of all three styles of teaching/learning.

Extracting Knowledge, Understanding, Wisdom

Knowledge		
Proverbs 18:15	**Proverbs 1:7**	**Proverbs 3:20**
The heart of the prudent getteth knowledge; and the ear of the wise seeketh knowledge.	The fear of the LORD is the beginning of knowledge; Fools despise wisdom and instruction.	By his knowledge the deeps broke open, and the clouds drop down the dew.

The Hebrew word for knowledge is דעת (*da'at*), which is derived from the parent root דע (*da*). The name of the Hebrew letter ד is *dalet*, from the Hebrew word דלת (*delet*) meaning "door." This letter was originally written as in the ancient pictographic script and is a picture of the tent door. In a previous discussion, we learned that this letter meant to "hang" as the door "hung" down from the roof of the tent. Each Hebrew letter has more than one meaning, and this letter can also mean back and forth or in and out movement as the door is used for moving in and out of the tent. The name of the Hebrew letter ע is *ayin*, from the Hebrew word עין (*ayin*) meaning "eye." This letter was originally written as in the ancient pictographic script and is a picture of an eye. When these two letters are combined, the Hebrew parent root דע (*dea*), is formed, meaning "the back, and forth movement of the eye." When something is carefully examined, one moves the eye back and forth to take in the whole of what is being examined. In the Ancient Hebrew mind, this careful examination is understood as knowledge and experience on an intimate level.

Do you know (yada) the balancings of the clouds, the wonderous works of complete knowledge (dea)? Job 37:16

The verb ידה (*Y.D.H*) is derived out of this parent root and carries this same meaning of an intimate knowledge. This verb is commonly used in, reference to the marital relations of a husband and wife.

And Adam knew Eve his wife; and she conceived, and bare Cain... Genesis 4:1 (KJV)

Do you know God? Not in the casual sense of awareness, as implied in the English sense of knowledge, but in a close and intimate relationship?

And those knowing your character will trust in you for you will not leave those seeking Yahweh. Psalm 9:11

God certainly knows us in this manner.

Will not God search this, for he knows the secrets of the heart. Psalm 44:21

Do we know God in this same manner? Do we know the heart of God?
And by this we may be sure that we know him, if we keep his commandments. 1 John 2:3 (RSV)

The above verse is being translated from a western perspective, but if we translate it through the mind of the Hebrews, we get a slightly different perspective.
And by this we may be sure that we have an intimate relationship with him if we preserve his directions.

Derived from the parent root דע (*da*) is the noun דעת (*da'at*), meaning "knowledge." The Hebrew word for knowledge is דעת (*da'at*), a noun derived from the verb ידע (*yada*) meaning "to know." The idea of "knowing" in Ancient Hebrew thought is like our understanding of knowing but is more personal and intimate. We may say that we "know" someone but simply mean we "know" of his or her existence but, in Hebrew thought one can only "know" someone if they have a personal and intimate relationship. In Genesis 18:19 God says about Abraham "I know him" meaning he has a very close relationship with Abraham. In Genesis 4:1 it says that Adam "knew Eve his wife" implying a very intimate sexual relationship.

Knowledge is the intimate ability to perform a specific task or function. This can be seen in Exodus chapter 31 where God had given men the ability to build the various furnishings of the tabernacle.

Source: Ancient Hebrew Research Center

Observation

Knowledge is basic human intellect retained through study, observation, and experience. In short, it is what we know. But biblical knowledge goes much deeper than that! It must be retained by an event called faith. What this means is you have to receive the information, and then believe the information. This is the starting line of faith, but faith is not complete until it has been applied. This is, why the Bible tells us that faith without works is dead.

How do you obtain knowledge?

It's simple. Just read the Bible. Be sure to study what you read and use a Concordance so that you can compare what you've read with other scriptures. Lastly, meditate on the Word of God. Meditation does not help you to believe what God said, but it does help you to remember what He said.

Understanding

Proverbs 4:7	Proverbs 3:5	Proverbs 20:5
And with all thy getting get understanding.	Trust in the LORD with all thine heart; and lean not unto thine own understanding.	Counsel in the heart of man is like deep water; but a man of understanding will draw it out.

The Hebrew word for understanding is תבון (*tavun*) comes from the verbal root בין (*biyn*) meaning to "understand" but the deeper meaning of this word can be found in a related verbal root - בנה (*banah*) which means to "build." In order, to build or construct something one must have the ability to plan and understand the processes needed. This is the idea behind the verb בין (*biyn*) and its derivative noun תבון (*tavun*), to be able to discern the processes of construction.

Source: Ancient Hebrew Research Center

Observation

To understand means to stand under or to submit to the Word of God by simply chewing the cud. This is what we call reflection. Meditation is absorbing or eating the Word, but reflection is regurgitating what you've eaten so that you can chew on it some more. This allows you to get all of the nutrients (revelation) out of what you've studied. All the same, understanding has levels, layers and compartments to it that can only be opened through an event called seeking. You seek after God's Word by showing up at Bible Study, getting yourself a mentor and asking questions. You then take the information that you've learned and compare it with other scriptures. Whenever possible, regurgitate that information again and chew on it some more until you've pretty much exhausted that scripture.

Wisdom

Proverbs 4:7	Proverbs 3:13	James 1:5
Wisdom is the principal thing; therefore get wisdom.	Happy is the man that findeth wisdom, and the man that getteth understanding.	If any of you lack wisdom, let him ask of God, that giveth to all men liberally, and upbraideth not; and it shall be given him.

The parent root חם (*hham*), meaning "heat," is the root of the word חכם (*hhakham*) which means "wisdom."

The word *hham* appears as in its original pictographic script. The letter is a picture of a wall which "separates" one side from another. And the letter is a picture of "water." Combined, these two letters literally mean "separate water." When "heat" (*hham*) is applied to water, we have evaporation, or a "separating of water."

The following Hebrew words are all derived from the parent root חם (*hham*).
חמת *hheymet* skin-bag חמה
- *hheymah* cheese חמ
- *hhammah* sun חמ
- *hhamas* to shake
- חמד *hhamad* to crave/desire חמ
- *hhamats* to sour

While we can plainly see the root חם (*hham*) at the beginning of each of these words, what may not be as plainly seen is how the meanings of each of these words are related.

Soured (חמץ) milk was placed in a skin-bag (חמת) that was set out in the heat (חם) of the sun (חמה) and shaken (חמס). The natural enzymes in the skin-bag causes the "water to separate" (חם) from the milk forming the delicacy (חמד) cheese (חמה).

So, what does all of this have to do with wisdom? חכם (*hhakham*) is related to the idea of "separating," as this word means "one who is able to separate between what is good and bad." This one word can be translated as either "skill" when applied to a craftsman, or as "wise" when applied to a leader or counselor.

and now send for me a man of skill (hhakham) to work in gold... 2 Chronicles 2:7

Provide for yourselves wise (hhakham) men and understanding and knowing for your tribes and I will set them as rulers over you. Deuteronomy 1:13

A verse found in the book of Isaiah has a very interesting connection between חמה (*hheymah* - cheese) and a חכם (*hhakham* - wisdom).

And he will eat cheese (hheymah) and honey (This Hebrew word can mean honey or dates) to know to reject the bad and choose the good. Isaiah 7:15

There appears to be a physical connection between cheese and wisdom as this passage indicates that eating cheese can bring about wisdom.

Source: Ancient Hebrew Research Center

Observation

Wisdom is the principal thing! This means that it is the most important of the three! But what exactly is wisdom? In short, it is applied knowledge that is now producing fruit in your life! God gives us knowledge, we pursue understanding until we overtake it, and then we give God back what we've learned. We don't do this just through words, but through teaching and demonstration. The first level of this process starts with knowledge. Knowledge leads us to acknowledge the motes or specks that we have in our own eyes. Understanding helps us to remove those planks, but wisdom means to break down those obstructions until they become fertilizer. We then take what knowledge and understanding produce in our lives and offer it back to God. This doesn't mean that we have to create an altar and start chanting; what it means is that we take what we've learned and apply it to our lives. Remember, obedience is better than sacrifice! As we walk out what we've learned, it produces friction, and that friction produces a sweet aroma of worship. The highest form of worship is submission! Those choices produce fruit, and that fruit is called wisdom!

Challenge

List three key differences between wisdom, knowledge and understanding.

Knowledge	Understanding	Wisdom

Why Should We Study the Word?

In truth, many believers do not like to read or study the Word of God. Don't get me wrong—they love the Lord, but our love for an individual can never go any further than our understanding of that person. Consequently, we have a lot of impotent Christians who claim Jesus as their Lord and Savior but do not personally know Him on an intimate level. So, whenever they face the inevitable storms of life, many of them are defeated; some even turn to false religions, while others turn completely away from anything that's faith-based (in the religious sense of the word). They'll proudly and angrily tell you how long they were Christians before they turned their backs on God, and they'll even tell you about the events that led up to them renouncing their faith. Nevertheless, what they won't tell you is this—they did not pursue God when they were professing Christians. Instead, they relied on their pastors to force-feed them scriptures every Sunday (or whenever they showed up for church). Again, when a storm came their way, they were unprepared. They prayed for the attack to end, but it only seemed to intensify until they began to lose things and people that were precious to them. This caused them to become angry with a God that they did not (personally) know and ultimately denounce Him as their God. Did they stop believing in Him? No, they didn't. Turning their backs on God was their attempt to "teach Him a lesson." Again, this is because they did not truly know Him, therefore, they humanized Him.

> **And even as they did not like to retain God in their knowledge, God gave them over to a reprobate mind, to do those things which are not convenient.**
> **Romans 1:28**

Consider this—in 2020, we all experienced a pandemic of epic proportions. We suddenly found ourselves facing what the World Health Organization coined as "COVID-19," also known as the Novel Coronavirus. Many people suffered losses as a result of the virus. To date, there have been over 500,000 COVID-related deaths in the United States alone! But what's not being reported is the number of marriages that have also perished as a result of the virus. This is because many people were forced to work from home alongside their spouses, and it was then that they discovered that they did not truly know (or like) their spouses. Hear me—this lack of knowledge stemmed from one of two facts:
   (a) They never truly knew their spouses.
   (b) They didn't know that their spouses had changed over the years.

Thankfully, God doesn't change; however, many of the religious divides that we see between believers and in our personal relationships with God has everything to do with our lack of knowledge regarding Him! When you do not truly know someone, you will misunderstand that person repeatedly. You will misinterpret their choices and their words, and you will find yourself becoming easily offended with them. You may even begin to abuse them by saying things that impact and trigger them in a negative way. This doesn't make you malicious, it simply means that you have separated yourself from that person by pursuing your own interests and not pursuing them. The same is true regarding our relationship with the Most High God. Matthew 7:7-8 says, "Ask, and it shall be given you; seek, and ye shall find; knock, and it shall be opened unto you: For everyone that asketh receiveth; and he that seeketh findeth; and to him that knocketh it shall be opened." Another scripture details the moment when many self-professing believers will stand before God, only to be turned away from Him. Their crime? They didn't know Him; consequently, He didn't know them. Matthew 7:21-23 details this event; it reads, "Not everyone that saith unto me, Lord, Lord, shall enter into the kingdom of heaven; but he that doeth the will of my Father which is in heaven. Many will say to me in that day, Lord, Lord, have we not prophesied in thy name? And in thy name have cast out devils? And in thy name done many wonderful works? And then will I profess unto them, I never knew you: depart from me, ye that work iniquity." Here, God is saying that these people did not pursue a relationship with Him. Instead, they were religious performers of miracles who sought after their own glory. This is why they didn't say, "Lord, I am yours. I have loved you and obeyed you for many years!" Instead, they were focused on their works, but God was focused on their hearts.

Romans 10:10
For with the heart man believeth unto righteousness; and with the mouth confession is made unto salvation.

So, why should we study the Word (often)?

1.	Jesus is the Living Word of God! We study the Word to get to know Him!
2.	To give Him the glory! When we know the Word, we can defeat the darts that Satan throws at us, thus allowing us to testify about victory after victory!
3.	To win souls for Christ.
4.	To show ourselves approved! But approved for what? Whatever it is that we've been praying and believing God for!
5.	To aid one another in prayer. "The effectual **fervent prayer** of a **righteous** man availeth much" (see James 5:16) and "How should one chase a thousand, and two put ten thousand to flight, except their Rock had sold them, and the LORD had shut them up?" (see Deuteronomy 32:30)
6.	To complete our assignments in the Earth.
7.	So that we can heal the sick, raise the dead and cast out devils!

Bible Journaling

Every day, we are bombarded with so much information that it becomes almost impossible for us to retain it all. It is for this reason that most of us suffer from "selective hearing." We instinctively gravitate towards and meditate on the information that we feel we need to accomplish our daily goals, but we store the rest of the information away in our conscious minds for later. And while we love the Lord, let us just be honest—we don't always place priority over His Word, especially when we are dealing with hardships. This is not to say that His Word isn't number one in our lives; it is to say that we oftentimes push it to the back of our minds so that we can complete the tasks at hand, and then once we've settled down, we'll sort through the information that we put away for later. That is, of course, if we don't forget it or, better yet, Satan doesn't snatch it.

Matthew 13:19
When anyone hears the word of the kingdom and does not understand it, the evil one comes and snatches away what has been sown in his heart.

To prevent this from happening, a great tool to use is Bible journaling. What is Bible journaling? A Bible journal is a hybrid of a diary coupled with Bible study notes. You can also use art, add prayers and jot down notes. The purpose of Bible journaling is to make the Bible more personal to you so that your devotional time can be more engaging and effective.

What You'll Need to Get Started
- Wide-Margin Bible or Journaling Bible (Paper or App)
- Journal or Notebook
- Writing Apparatus

Note: some people write and draw on the pages of their Bibles, while others prefer to use a separate journal or notebook. Of course, this is totally up to you!

Benefits of Bible Journaling

Improved Focus: Bible journaling helps you to focus more on the scriptures instead of reading while distracted.

Improved Memory: Better focus equates to better Word retention!

An Ever-Growing Faith: Better word retention equates to a faith that keeps expanding!

Open Heavens: Great faith means that you are in alignment with God, and therefore, no (good) thing that you desire can or will be withheld from you!

Kingdom Authority on Earth: Kingdom authority is the ability to bring Heaven to Earth, not just through material abundance, but through the demonstration of signs, miracles, and wonders.

Tips for Basic Bible Journaling

1. Pray first! This is self-explanatory, but before communing with God, it is always best to pray first.
2. Date each entry. This will allow you to keep track of each occurrence so that you can reflect on it later.
3. Read and reflect on a passage of scripture.
4. Pick out the words in that passage that stand out to you. Write them down in your journal.
5. Visualize these words. For example, you can draw images that relate to some of the highlighted words.
6. Next, write a Bible story or a personal testimony that relates to that story.
7. Optional: Add layers to your journal by writing prayers or listing how you plan to activate some of the words you've highlighted in your life on that day.

Extra Creative Bible Journaling

What You'll Need to Get Started
- Wide-Margin Bible or Journaling Bible (Paper or App)
- Journal or Notebook
- Post-It™ Notes (small)
- Post-It™ Notes (standard-sized)
- Highlighters
- Stickers

Tips

1. For extra-creative journaling, follow the tips/steps above, but to make the experience more memorable, simply use Post-It tabs to bookmark the pages that you were reading.
2. Be sure to post the passages on the tabs; this way, they'll be easier to find, especially if you like to mark up your Bible. Also, be sure to organize the tabs; for example, you can use green tabs to represent money, success, and everything related to material abundance. You can use the yellow tabs to represent yielding, obeying God, and self-control.
3. Highlight the passages that stand out to you the most. To make it easier to find the passages, use different color highlighters to highlight the text.
4. Use standard-size Post-It™ or sticky notes to write additional notes and prayers.
5. Use stickers for more of a creative flare!

Alphabetize Your Study Time

I have created an Alphabet System to help you to maximize your study time and extract the most benefits from it. Whenever you are studying a specific subject (i.e., fear, rejection, peace), list the subject next to the corresponding alphabet. The following chart already has a list of subjects for you to study. Be sure to dedicate time to studying these subjects. On the next page, you will find an empty chart for you to fill in.

A	**Antichrist**	
B	**Baptism**	
C	**Condemnation**	
D	**Demon**	
E	**Exhortation**	
F	**Faith**	
G	**Gentleness**	
H	**Hope**	
I	**Introspection**	
J	**Joy**	
K	**Kindness**	
L	**Love**	
M	**Meekness**	

N	**Nation**	
O	**Omnipotence**	
P	**Patience**	
Q	**Quarrel**	
R	**Redemption**	
S	**Salvation**	
T	**Test/Trials**	
U	**Unforgiveness**	
V	**Victory**	
W	**Worship**	
X		
Y	**Yoke**	
Z	**Zeal**	

I have created an Alphabet System to help you to maximize your study time and extract the most benefits from it. Whenever you are studying a specific subject (i.e., fear, rejection, peace), list the subject next to the corresponding alphabet.

A		
B		
C		
D		
E		
F		
G		
H		
I		
J		
K		
L		
M		
N		
O		

P		
Q		
R		
S		
T		
U		
V		
W		
X		
Y		
Z		

List of Bible Symbols

The following lists were taken from Bible Gateway

Symbolic Objects		
Symbol	Meaning	Scriptures
The Rainbow	Symbol of God's Covenant	Ge 9:13; Eze 1:28; Rev 4:3
Stairway	Symbol of the Way to God	Ge 28:11-13; Jn 1:51
Thunder, Lightning, Cloud and Smoke	Symbols of God's Majesty	Ex 19:16-18; Ex 24:17; Ps 97:2,4; Rev 4:5; Rev 8:5; Rev 11:19
Thunder	Symbol of God's Voice	Ps 29:3; Ps 68:33
Trumpets	Symbol of God Speaking	Ex 19:19; Rev 8:6
Pillar of Cloud and Fire	Symbol of Guidance	Ex 13:21
Throne	Symbol of God's Glory	Isa 6:1; Eze 1:26; Rev 4:2; Rev 22:3
Dry Bones	Symbol of Spiritual Death	Eze 37:1-2,11
White Hair	Symbol of Wisdom	Da 7:9; Rev 1:14
Wind	Symbol of the Holy Spirit	Jn 3:8; Ac 2:2
Fire	Symbol of the Holy Spirit	Ac 2:3
Stars and Lampstands	Symbols of God's Ministers	Rev 1:20
Signet Ring	Symbol of Authority	Est 8:10; Hag 2:23
Arrows	Symbols of God's Judgments	Ps 38:2; Ps 120:4
Sceptre	Symbol of God's Rule	Ps 2:9; Rev 2:27; Rev 19:15
Capstone	Symbol of Pre-eminence	Mt 21:42 pp Mk 12:10-11 pp Lk 20:17; Ps 118:22
Rock	Symbol of Stability	Ps 18:2; Ps 40:2
Human Body	Symbol of Interdependence	1Co 12:27
Grass	Symbol of Human Frailty	Ps 90:5-6; 1Pe 1:24

Symbolic Creatures		
Serpent	Symbol of Satan's Subtlety	Ge 3:1; Rev 12:9; Rev 20:1-3
Locusts	Symbol of God's Judgment	Ex 10:12; Joel 1:4; Rev 9:3
Beasts	Symbols of Earthly Kingdoms	Da 7:2-7,17; Da 8:20-22
A dove	Symbol of the Holy Spirit	Mt 3:16 pp Mk 1:10 pp Lk 3:22
Lamb	Symbol of Jesus Christ's Sacrifice	Rev 5:6

Symbolic Actions		
Breaking a Jar	Symbol of the Destruction of Jerusalem	Jer. 19:10-11
Cursing of a Fig Tree	Symbol of Judgment	Mt 21:18-19 pp Mk 11:12-14
Washing Hands	Symbol of Innocence	Mt 27:24
Being Thirsty	Symbol of Spiritual Need	Ps 63:1; Jn 7:37
Baptism	Symbol of Salvation in Jesus Christ	Ac 22:16; Ro 6:3-4; 1Pe 3:21
The Lord's Supper	Symbol of Union with Christ	Mt 26:26-29 pp Mk 14:22-24 pp Lk 22:19-20 pp 1Co 11:23-26
Anointing	Symbol of Empowering by God's Spirit	1Sa 16:13; Lk 4:18; Isa 61:1
Harvesting	Symbol of Judgment Day	Joel 3:12-13; Mt 13:29-30; Rev 14:15
Tearing Garments	Symbol of Anger and Sorrow	Ge 37:29,34; Jos 7:6
Spitting	Symbol of Contempt	Isa 50:6; Mt 26:67 pp Mk 14:65
Shaking Off Dust	Symbol of Rejection	Mt 10:14 pp Lk 9:5; Ac 13:51
Sitting in Sackcloth and Ashes	Symbol of Repentance	Ps 69:11; Isa 22:12; Jnh 3:5-6; Mt 11:21
Lifting of Hands	Symbol of Prayer	Ps 63:4; 1Ti 2:8
Covering the Head	Symbol of Submission	1Co 11:3-10

List of Bible Symbols

Symbols Expressing God's Nature and Character		
God's Face	Symbol of His Presence	Nu 6:25-26; Ps 34:16
God's Arm or Hand	Symbol of His Power	Ps 21:8; Ps 89:13
God's Eyes	Symbol of His Awareness	Pr. 15:3; 1Pe 3:12
God's Ear	Symbol of God Listening	Ps 31:2; Isa 59:1

Source: Bible Gateway

Bible Book Abbreviations

Book	Most Common Abbreviation
Genesis	Gen.
Exodus	Ex.
Leviticus	Lev.
Numbers	Num.
Deuteronomy	Deut.
Joshua	Josh.
Judges	Judg.
Ruth	Ruth
1 Samuel	1 Sam.
2 Samuel	2 Sam.
1 Kings	1 Kings
2 Kings	2 Kings
1 Chronicles	1 Chron.
2 Chronicles	2 Chron.
Ezra	Ezra
Nehemiah	Neh.
Esther	Est.
Job	Job
Psalms	Ps.
Proverbs	Prov.
Ecclesiastes	Eccles.
Song of Solomon	Song
Isaiah	Isa.
Jeremiah	Jer.
Lamentations	Lam.
Ezekiel	Ezek.
Daniel	Dan.
Hosea	Hos.
Joel	Joel

Book	Most Common Abbreviation
Amos	Amos
Obadiah	Obad.
Jonah	Jonah
Micah	Mic.
Nahum	Nah.
Habakkuk	Hab.
Zephaniah	Zeph.
Haggai	Hag.
Zechariah	Zech.
Malachi	Mal.
Matthew	Matt.
Mark	Mark
Luke	Luke
John	John
Acts	Acts
Romans	Rom.
1 Corinthians	1 Cor.
2 Corinthians	2 Cor.
Galatians	Gal.
Ephesians	Eph.
Philippians	Phil.
Colossians	Col.
1 Thessalonians	1 Thess.
2 Thessalonians	2 Thess.
1 Timothy	1 Tim.
2 Timothy	2 Tim.
Titus	Titus
Philemon	Philem.
Hebrews	Heb.
James	James
1 Peter	1 Pet.

Book	Most Common Abbreviation
2 Peter	2 Pet.
1 John	1 John
2 John	2 John
3 John	3 John
Jude	Jude
Revelation	Rev.

The Foundations of Faith

What exactly is faith?
Before we delve deep into the topic of faith, let us look at the etymology of the word.

Faith
mid-13c., faith, feith, fei, fai "faithfulness to a trust or promise; loyalty to a person; honesty, truthfulness," from Anglo-French and Old French feid, foi "faith, belief, trust, confidence; pledge" (11c.), from Latin fides "trust, faith, confidence, reliance, credence, belief," from root of fidere "to trust,"from PIE root *bheidh- "to trust, confide, persuade." For sense evolution, see belief. Accommodated to other English abstract nouns in -th (truth, health, etc.). From early 14c. as "assent of the mind to the truth of a statement for which there is incomplete evidence," especially "belief in religious matters" (matched with hope and charity). Since mid-14c. in reference, to the Christian church or religion; from late 14c. in reference, to any religious persuasion.   And faith is neither the submission of the reason, nor is it the acceptance, simply and absolutely upon testimony, of what reason cannot reach. Faith is, the being able to cleave to a power of goodness appealing to our higher and real self, not to our lower and apparent self. [Matthew Arnold, "Literature & Dogma," 1873] From late 14c. as "confidence in a person or thing with reference to truthfulness or reliability," also "fidelity of one spouse to another." Also, in Middle English "a sworn oath," hence its frequent use in Middle English oaths and asseverations (par ma fay, mid-13c.; bi my fay, c. 1300).
Source: Online Etymology Dictionary

As you can see, there are seven pillars or foundations that come together to build the structure of faith. They are:

1. Trust
2. Loyalty (Consistency)
3. Confidence
4. Intimacy
5. Hope
6. Charity
7. A Promise

If any of these components are missing, it perverts the faith; this is what births what we oftentimes refer to as religiousness. To be religious (outside of a relationship with God) simply means to be ritualistic or better yet, perform the acts of a priest without having the heart of God.

It means to be transactional, expecting God to repay you for your obedience; it is pretty much trying to provoke God to perform for a few bucks or a few hours of your time. This is what I call the Genie in a Bottle syndrome that many believers suffer from. We'll delve more into that shortly, but let's look at the seven pillars of faith a little more.

Trust
Definition: Firm belief in the reliability, truth, ability, or strength of someone or something.
Source: Oxford Languages

The Greek word for "trust" is "pistis" and it literally means to be persuaded. But how can you be persuaded regarding things you cannot see? The answer is simple; you study the Word of God and pray. This is what the Bible refers to as "seeking." Matthew 7:7 reads, "Ask, and it shall be given you; seek, and ye shall find; knock, and it shall be opened unto you." When you have an appetite for the truth, God will fill that appetite if you ask Him.

Loyalty
Definition: the quality of staying firm in your friendship or support for someone or something.
Source: Collins Dictionary

Another word for "loyalty" is consistency. It means to be reliable, trustworthy, and relatively predictable as it relates to your commitment to a person or vow. It also means to be faithful or, better yet, full of faith.

Confidence
Definition: the feeling or belief that one can rely on someone or something; firm trust.
Source: Oxford Languages

Of course, another word for "confidence" is trust. To trust means to lean to or depend on something or someone based solely on a belief that what or who you're leaning on or trusting in can support you in that area. The basis for your belief could be:
- the words of the person you're trusting in.
- the words of whomever it was that referred you to that person.
- the advertisement of a product or service through word of mouth or media.
- your history with that individual.
- your history with whatever it is that you're trusting in.

To have confidence in a person or thing means that you can fully surrender to whatever or whomever it is that you're trusting, especially regarding something that is important or sensitive to you, without attempting to micromanage the event. It means to know or be fully convinced that the person or the thing will be able to carry out a specific function in excellence.

Intimacy
Definition: the state of having a close personal relationship with somebody.
Source: Oxford Learner's Dictionaries

Another word for "intimate" is "familiar," and as you can see, the word "familiar" comes from the word "family." In human relationships, our families are oftentimes the people who we are most intimate with. This means that we readily and freely share information with them that we wouldn't share with anyone else; we show them sides of ourselves that we won't reveal to anyone else. This is the nature of intimacy; it means to reveal and, of course, to reveal something that is sacred, personal, or even humiliating requires a certain level of trust. If you share a secret with a person, it means that you are (in that moment) confident that the individual will guard your secret and not share it with anyone else.

Hope
Definition: a feeling of expectation and desire for a certain thing to happen.
Source: Oxford Languages

Hope is very similar to faith; as a matter of fact, it is one of the components or ingredients of faith. Hope is the umbilical cord that connects an individual to Heaven, allowing that individual to download whatever it is that he or she is believing God for. Think of it this way—whenever you pull into a service station to refuel your vehicle, you must pull up close to a fuel pump. Why do you go to the gas station? Because you have a need and you trust that they will be able to fulfill that specific need. When you pull in next to a pump, you're simply getting in position to replenish that need. Next, you'll either pay at the pump or go into the station to pay for your fuel before pumping it. And finally, you'll lift the nozzle of the gas pump and plug it into your vehicle. Everything you did at that station was driven by hope. Get this—there is no guarantee that the pump you're using will work; you simply believe that it will work because of word of mouth and because it has worked in the past. This is a picture of hope. It means to get in position; this movement or positioning is driven by expectation. The Greek word for "hope" is "elpis" and it literally means "expectation."

Charity
Definition: benevolent goodwill toward or love of humanity.
Source: Oxford Languages

The word "charity" is oftentimes used synonymously with "love," and its Greek counterpart, amazingly enough, is "agape." Agape means "love" or "goodwill." This is what activates faith; it is the driving force or the "why" behind the "what." Going back to the gas station example, it is the pressure you put on the lever, forcing the tank to release a measure of fuel. Of course, the amount of fuel it releases is mainly determined by the amount of pressure you put on the lever and, of course, the size of the nozzle itself. And it goes without saying that since God is inexhaustible, what we pull out of Heaven solely depends on the size of our faith.

A Promise
Definition: a declaration or assurance that one will do a particular thing or that a particular thing will happen.
Source: Oxford Languages

In order for us to have a gas pump, we have to have something to connect it to. This is what we call faith. Faith is the vehicle that we empower, but in order for faith to be complete, it must have a driving force behind its wheel. This is what we call the promise. What this means is that we aren't driving or traveling towards a specific thing or event; the ultimate goal is that we become more like Christ, but what often motivates us, on the other hand, are things and events.

The Sizes of Faith

Little Faith	Strong Faith	Great Faith
"If God so clothes the grass of the field, which today is, and tomorrow is thrown into the oven, will He not much more clothe you, O you of little faith?" (Matthew 6:30) "But He said to them, 'Why are you fearful, O you of little	"He staggered not at the promise of God through unbelief; but was strong in faith, giving glory to God." (Romans 4:20) "For though I be absent in the flesh, yet am I with you in the spirit, joying and beholding your order, and the	"When Jesus heard it, He marveled, and said to those who followed, "Assuredly, I say to you, I have not found such great faith, not even in Israel!" (Matthew 8:8-10) "...O woman, great is your faith! Let it be to you as you desire..."

Little Faith	Strong Faith	Great Faith
faith?' Then He arose and rebuked the winds and the sea, and there was a great calm. (Matthew 8:26)	stedfastness of your faith in Christ." (Colossians 2:5)	(Matthew 15:21-28)

What's the difference between little faith, strong faith, and great faith?

Little Faith
Little faith is just that … it is small in proportion. It is (or should be) the faith of a beginner; this is because a new believer does not (consciously) have a lot of history with God. Consequently, the new beginner will often have small faith. Nevertheless, Jesus told us that this is enough to move mountains. (Luke 17:6: And the Lord said, If ye had faith as a grain of mustard seed, ye might say unto this sycamine tree, Be thou plucked up by the root, and be thou planted in the sea; and it should obey you.)

Strong Faith
Strong faith is faith that is resistant to the many opposing forces that come up against it. It means to be steadfast, unmovable, and always abounding in the work of the Lord. This is the type of faith that Apostle Paul spoke of in Galatians 6:9, which reads, "And let us not be weary in well doing: for in due season we shall reap, if we faint not." This is a faith that is stubborn, a faith that is so anchored in the Word of God that it remains stable and consistent, even in the harshest of storms.

Great Faith
Great faith is faith that reaches beyond the individual who possesses it and is able to affect others; it means that the individual has yielded himself or herself as a conduit for faith to pass through. This is the type of faith that allows us to heal the sick, cast out devils, and raise the dead.

The Pulse of Faith

James 2:14-17

What doth it profit, my brethren, though a man say he hath faith, and have not works? Can faith save him? If a brother or sister be naked, and destitute of daily food, and one of you say unto them, Depart in peace, be ye warmed and filled; notwithstanding ye give them not those things which are needful to the body; what doth it profit? Even so faith if it hath not works, is dead, being alone.

Let us go back to the gas station example. Imagine that you've filled your car up with gas, you've paid the price for the fuel, and now, you're sitting behind the wheel of your car. Your hands are on the steering wheel, but you have not started the car, nor are you driving it. After having paid tens of thousands of dollars for the car that you're driving, you'd think that it would do the next sensible thing, and that is to drive itself! Nevertheless, your vehicle does not have a brain! Regardless of the many advances in technology that we see surfacing everyday, there is no technology that would allow us to (safely) drive a car through a sea of traffic. Don't get me wrong; new advances in technology allowed us to create cars that are capable of driving without a human being behind the wheel, but get this—a human has to be involved in the process, even if that human is driving the car virtually! This is because people are unpredictable, and so is nature. So right now, we still need people to man or manage the four to eight-thousand pound metal containers that we call vehicles. This means that even though you put gas in the vehicle, the vehicle still needs your energy to operate. It needs you to crank it up, put it in gear and navigate it from one place to another. In order, for you to do this, you need to be sober-minded, have a destination in mind, and you must know the route to get you to that destination. This means that James 2:14-17 was simply telling us that faith without our own investments (time, sweat, blood, effort) is like a parked vehicle. While it may have the fuel, it is missing one of the most important components: human will!

All too often, we (as believers) claim to have faith; we pray for something to come to pass, and then we wait for it to come to pass. Let us look at the chasm between praying and receiving, and let's juxtapose that with the Israelites' journey from Egypt to the Promised Land.

Wrong Way		
Prayer	Waiting	Reception/Possession
Egypt	Wilderness	Promised Land

Right Way		
Prayer	Works (Walking/Moving)	Reception/Possession
Egypt	Wilderness	Promised Land

Imagine it this way—the people of God were the fuel that God was trying to deliver to the Promised Land, but while putting pressure on the lever, He noticed that nothing was coming out. He looked, into the nozzle and noticed that the people were all gathering around each other, trying to keep warm. No one was moving forward; instead, they were all waiting. If He placed that nozzle back on the gas pump, they'd still be waiting, right?! This means that they could not be passive in their own deliverance! They had to put forth effort and energy to not only come out of Egypt, but to also come out of the wilderness! Waiting clogs the lines between Heaven and Earth, therefore, the pulse of faith is human will or, better yet, works!

Pillars of Faith (Synonyms)

To better understand each pillar, study the synonyms below. Be sure to research each word and incorporate that word into your life and your lifestyle.

Trust						
Confidence	Expect	Hope	Assurance	Certainty	Accredit	Assume
Presume	Suppose	Take	Surmise	Rely On	Build On	Swear By
Lean To	Account	Credence	Bet On	Depend On	Accept	Belief

Loyalty						
Allegiance	Devotion	Obedience	Reliability	Integrity	Fidelity	Govern
Honesty	Honor	Support	Faith	Bond	Faithfulness	Adhere to
Commit	Obligate	Firm	Steadfast	Trustworthy	Resolute	Unwavering

Confidence				
Assurance	Faith	Hope	Courage	Tenacity
Certainty	Determination	Grit	Reliance	Self-Possession
Firmness	Trust	Dependence	Stock	Boldness

Intimacy

Affection	Confidence	Familiarity	Acquaintance	Experience
Confidentiality	Friendship	Relationship	Understanding	Closeness
Communion	Affinity	Togetherness	Oneness	Rapport

Hope

Ambition	Expectation	Faith	Belief	Desire	Confidence	Concern
Anticipation	Aspiration	Wish	Cherish	Assume	Foresee	Contemplate
Hold Fast	Rely	Await	Suppose	Surmise	Endure	Goal

Charity

Agape	Affection	Benevolence	Generosity	Humanity
Amity	Goodness	Clemency	Alms	Mercy
Grace	Goodwill	Relieve	Assist	Love

Promise

Agreement	Assurance	Commit	Guarantee	Bond	Obligate	Betroth
Pact	Pledge	Oath	Vow	Word	Contract	Swear
Consent	Affirm	Covenant	Insurance	Espouse	Stipulate	Warranty

Abraham, the Father of Faith

Romans 4:16-25

Therefore it is of faith, that it might be by grace; to the end the promise might be sure to all the seed; not to that only which is of the law, but to that also which is of the faith of Abraham; who is the father of us all, (As it is written, I have made thee a father of many nations,) before him whom he believed, even God, who quickeneth the dead, and calleth those things which be not as though they were. Who against hope believed in hope, that he might become the father of many nations; according to that which was spoken, So shall thy seed be. And being not weak in faith, he considered not his own body now dead, when he was about an hundred years old, neither yet the deadness of Sara's womb: He staggered not at the promise of God through unbelief; but was strong in faith, giving glory to God; And being fully persuaded that, what he had promised, he was able also to perform. And therefore it was imputed to him for

> righteousness. Now it was not written for his sake alone, that it was imputed to him; but for us also, to whom it shall be imputed, if we believe on him that raised up Jesus our Lord from the dead; who was delivered for our offenses, and was raised again for our justification.

A father, biblically speaking, is a spiritual foundation by which a lineage is established. Abraham is considered by three faiths to be the father of faith because of his great faith (which still continues across the spectrum of faiths to this day) and God's declaration regarding him.

The three Abrahamic faiths are:

Christianity	Judaism	Islam

This means that Abraham's faith and his story are great pillars within these faiths. Nevertheless, let us study the man himself!

Original Name: Abram

Spouses		
Sarah	Hagar	Keturah

Note: Many theologians, scholars, historians, and the like believe that Keturah and Hagar are the same person. Proponents for the two-wife theory cite Genesis 25:1, which states, "Then again Abraham took a wife, and her name was Keturah." Other biblical translations say it this way—"Abraham took another wife, whose name was Keturah." The word "another" implies that Abraham had another wife in addition to Keturah. 1 Chronicles 1:32 refers to Keturah as a concubine which, of course, was a woman who often served as a handmaiden to her master/husband's wife. A concubine was oftentimes a slave or a servant who acted as a second-class wife. 1 Chronicles 1:32 reads, "Now the sons of Keturah, Abraham's concubine: she bare Zimran, and Jokshan, and Medan, and Midian, and Ishbak, and Shuah." Opponents of this theory, however, cite Genesis 25:6, which reads, "But unto the sons of the concubines, which Abraham had, Abraham gave gifts, and sent them away from Isaac his son, while he yet lived, eastward, unto the east country." This means that in addition to Sarah, Abraham had (at least) two other wives. Supporters of the two-wife theory believe that God changed Hagar's name because of her faith and obedience to Him while in the wilderness. Because of her faith, like Sarah, her name was changed. They even use the fact that Ishmael (Abraham's son with Hagar) was present at his funeral. "And his sons Isaac and Ishmael buried him in the cave of Machpelah, in the field of Ephron the son of Zohar the Hittite, which is before Mamre; the field which Abraham purchased of the sons of Heth: there was Abraham buried, and Sarah his wife"

(Genesis 25:9-10). Non-supporters of this theory point out the fact that the Bible named Keturah's sons without mentioning Ishmael, plus, the Bible makes no mention of Keturah's heritage. We do know that she was a concubine, but the text would suggest that Abraham had a monogamous relationship with her up until his death at the age of 175.

The Faith of Abraham

Genesis 22:1-19

And it came to pass after these things, that God did tempt Abraham, and said unto him, Abraham: and he said, Behold, here I am. And he said, Take now thy son, thine only son Isaac, whom thou lovest, and get thee into the land of Moriah; and offer him there for a burnt offering upon one of the mountains which I will tell thee of. And Abraham rose up early in the morning, and saddled his ass, and took two of his young men with him, and Isaac his son, and clave the wood for the burnt offering, and rose up, and went unto the place of which God had told him. Then on the third day Abraham lifted up his eyes, and saw the place afar off. And Abraham said unto his young men, Abide ye here with the ass; and I and the lad will go yonder and worship, and come again to you. And Abraham took the wood of the burnt offering, and laid it upon Isaac his son; and he took the fire in his hand, and a knife; and they went both of them together. And Isaac spake unto Abraham his father, and said, My father: and he said, Here am I, my son. And he said, Behold the fire and the wood: but where is the lamb for a burnt offering? And Abraham said, My son, God will provide himself a lamb for a burnt offering: so they went both of them together.
And they came to the place which God had told him of; and Abraham built an altar there, and laid the wood in order, and bound Isaac his son, and laid him on the altar upon the wood. And Abraham stretched forth his hand, and took the knife to slay his son.
And the angel of the LORD called unto him out of heaven, and said, Abraham, Abraham: and he said, Here am I. And he said, Lay not thine hand upon the lad, neither do thou any thing unto him: for now I know that thou fearest God, seeing thou hast not withheld thy son, thine only son from me. And Abraham lifted up his eyes, and looked, and behold behind him a ram caught in a thicket by his horns: and Abraham went and took the ram, and offered him up for a burnt offering in the stead of his son. And Abraham called the name of that place Jehovahjireh: as it is said to this day, In the mount of the LORD it shall be seen.
And the angel of the LORD called unto Abraham out of heaven the second time, And said, By myself have I sworn, saith the LORD, for because thou hast done this thing, and hast not withheld thy son, thine only son: That in blessing I will bless thee, and in multiplying I will multiply thy seed as the stars of the heaven, and as the sand which is upon the sea shore; and thy seed shall possess the gate of his enemies; And in thy seed shall all the nations of the earth be blessed; because thou hast obeyed my voice. So Abraham returned unto his young men, and they rose up and went together to Beersheba; and Abraham dwelt at Beersheba.

Let us look at the highlighted portions of the text.
- God tempted Abraham. The word "tempt" here simply means that God tested Abraham.
- God referred to Isaac as Abraham's only son, even though we know that Abraham fathered Ishmael with Hagar. This was because Isaac was the son of promise; he was a product of great faith, whereas Ishmael had been a product of little faith. He was born as a response to Abraham and Sarah's attempt to bring the prophetic word regarding them having a son to pass because Sarah thought she was too old to bare children.
- Reading this text, we could all assume that Abraham did not love his son, Ishmael, but this is not what this text meant. It simply means favor. Abraham favored Isaac because he was the son of promise. Additionally, Isaac was Abraham's son with Sarah, a woman whom he loved dearly.
- There were five types of offerings in the Old Testament. Abraham was commanded to offer Isaac as a burnt offering.

Five Types of Offerings				
Burnt Offerings	**Grain Offerings**	**Peace Offerings**	**Sin Offerings**	**Guilt Offerings**
Leviticus 1	Leviticus 2	Leviticus 3,7	Leviticus 4	Leviticus 5

Burnt Offering Ritual
Leviticus 1:1-9
And the LORD called unto Moses, and spake unto him out of the tabernacle of the congregation, saying, speak unto the children of Israel, and say unto them, If any man of you bring an offering unto the LORD, ye shall bring your offering of the cattle, even of the herd, and of the flock. If his offering be a burnt sacrifice of the herd, let him offer a male without blemish: he shall offer it of his own voluntary will at the door of the tabernacle of the congregation before the LORD. And he shall put his hand upon the head of the burnt offering; and it shall be accepted for him to make atonement for him. And he shall kill the bullock before the LORD: and the priests, Aaron's sons, shall bring the blood, and sprinkle the blood round about upon the altar that is by the door of the tabernacle of the congregation. And he shall flay the burnt offering, and cut it into his pieces. And the sons of Aaron the priest shall put fire upon the altar, and lay the wood in order upon the fire: And the priests, Aaron's sons, shall lay the parts, the head, and the fat, in order upon the wood that is on the fire which is upon the altar: But his inwards and his legs shall he wash in water: and the priest shall burn all on the altar, to be a burnt sacrifice, an offering made by fire, of a sweet savor unto the LORD.

Why is this significant? It shows the brutality that Abraham would have had to inflict upon his son. This is, why Isaac was a type and shadow of Jesus Christ.
- Abraham rose early in the morning.
- Abraham went to the place where God told him. We see this pattern in Abraham's life throughout the Bible. He trusted God and went wherever He told him to go. This was an act of obedience, and obedience is the highest expression of faith.
- Abraham took the wood for the burnt offering and laid it upon his son, Isaac. Wood, in the scriptures, is used to symbolize flesh. Again, he is a type and shadow of Christ. Jesus bore our sins in His body just as Isaac bore the wood that his father placed on his back.
- Abraham stretched forth his hand and took the knife to slay his son. Faith without works is dead! In that moment, Abraham's faith was activated, and Heaven had to respond!
- Here am I. This is just another way of saying, "Here I am" or "Here, I Am." Who is God? In the book of Revelations, He refers to Himself as "The Great I Am." What does this mean? It's simple:

(1). He is Truth! (2). He cannot tell a lie! (3). He is!

Think of it this way—everything that God says has to obey Him, so if God said that the cover of this book is black, it would immediately become just that—black! Everything He says is, meaning, it exists the minute He says it. Everything God says about Himself is true because He is Truth; this is, why He is I Am! When Abraham said, "Here I am," he was simply saying that he was within the perimeters of God's will. This is a far cry from the event that took place in Eden when Adam and Eve hid themselves from God, meaning, they were outside of God's will. When God went looking for them, He asked, "Where art thou?" or "Where are you?" In other words, God could not find the couple inside His will, because they could no longer relate to Him. Amos 3:3 says, "Can two walk together except they agreed?" Nevertheless, Abraham managed to (somewhat) repair the breach that had been created between God and mankind through Adam's sin. And while he could not serve as a bridge between Heaven and Hell, men and women of faith would find themselves resting in what the Bible refers to as Abraham's bosom upon their deaths. This kept them from the lake of fire and served as a temporary resting place until the death and resurrection of Jesus Christ. We see the evidence of this in the story of the rich man who went to Hell. Please note that this story, unlike many stories shared in the Bible, was not a parable; it was an actual event that took place.

Luke 16:19-31

There was a certain rich man, which was clothed in purple and fine linen, and fared

> sumptuously every day: And there was a certain beggar named Lazarus, which was laid at his gate, full of sores, and desiring to be fed with the crumbs which fell from the rich man's table: moreover the dogs came and licked his sores. **And it came to pass, that the beggar died, and was carried by the angels into Abraham's bosom:** the rich man also died, and was buried; And in Hell he lift up his eyes, being in torments, **and seeth Abraham afar off, and Lazarus in his bosom**. And he cried and said, Father Abraham, have mercy on me, and send Lazarus, that he may dip the tip of his finger in water, and cool my tongue; for I am tormented in this flame. But Abraham said, Son, remember that thou in thy lifetime receivedst thy good things, and likewise Lazarus evil things: but now he is comforted, and thou art tormented. And beside all this, **between us and you there is a great gulf fixed**: so that they which would pass from hence to you cannot; neither can they pass to us, that would come from thence. Then he said, I pray thee therefore, father, that thou wouldest send him to my father's house: For I have five brethren; that he may testify unto them, lest they also come into this place of torment. Abraham saith unto him, They have Moses and the prophets; let them hear them. And he said, Nay, father Abraham: but if one went unto them from the dead, they will repent. And he said unto him, If they hear not Moses and the prophets, neither will they be persuaded, though one rose from the dead.

What this means is that Abraham had great faith! His faith not only served as a conduit between himself and God, but it also helped many others to find their way back to God through faith.

Other Facts About Abraham
1. Abraham was a tenth-generation descendant of Noah.
2. Abraham's parents were idol-worshipers.
3. Abraham's name means "father of a multitude."
4. Abram was 75-years old when God told him to leave Ur.
5. Abraham was 86-years old when Ishmael was born.
6. Abraham was 100-years old when Isaac was born.
7. The Bible did not mention Abraham's other six sons being present at his burial, only Isaac and Ishmael.
8. Technically speaking, Abraham did not lie about Sarah being his sister. In Genesis 20:12-13, he explained to Abimelech, king of Gerar, that Sarah was the daughter of his father but not the daughter of his mother.

9. Abraham's bosom was a temporary compartment in Hell where the righteous were housed prior to Jesus' death and resurrection. When the Bible talks about the saints who came out of their graves and were seen when Jesus gave up His ghost, these are the souls who the Bible was referring to. This is what the Bible means when it says, "When he ascended up on high, he led captivity captive, and gave gifts unto men."

Faith Scriptures

Hebrews 11:1
Now faith is the substance of things hoped for, the evidence of things not seen.

Hebrews 11:6
And without faith it is impossible to please him, for whoever would draw near to God must believe that he exists and that he rewards those who seek him.

Ephesians 2:8-9
For by grace are ye saved through faith; and that not of yourselves: it is the gift of God: Not of works, lest any man should boast.

1 John 5:4
For everyone who has been born of God overcomes the world. And this is the victory that has overcome the world—our faith.

Romans 10:17
So, faith comes from hearing, and hearing through the word of Christ.

2 Corinthians 5:7
For we walk by faith, not by sight.

Mark 16:16
Whoever believes and is baptized will be saved, but whoever does not believe will be condemned.

Matthew 21:22
And whatever you ask in prayer, you will receive, if you have faith.

THE FACE OF GOD

2 Chronicles 7:14
If my people who are called by my name humble themselves, and pray and seek my face and turn from their wicked ways, then I will hear from heaven and will forgive their sin and heal their land.

Exodus 33:20
But," he said, "you cannot see my face, for man shall not see me and live."

Numbers 6:25-26
The Lord make His face shine on you, and be gracious to you; the Lord lift up His countenance on you, and give you peace.'

When we think about the word "face," we often imagine a human being, complete with eyes, eyebrows, a nose, a mouth, and teeth. But God is Spirit; this is why we must worship Him in Spirit and in Truth. He is not human, so how is it that the Bible describes Him as having the features of a man? All the same, we were created in His image. Does this mean that we were created to look like Him? The simple answer is—we are humans, limited in our knowledge of the natural realm. We cannot comprehend spiritual things, therefore, to help us to get to know Him more, God describes Himself using words that we can relate to. Howbeit, the face of God (as used in the scriptures) represents the mind, the heart, and the will of God. We are made in His image, just not in a natural sense. Nevertheless, the Bible is replete with scriptures that use physical or natural terminology to describe the Most High God.

The Hair of God	The Shape of God	The Countenance of God
Daniel 7:9	John 5:37	Psalm 11:7
I beheld till the thrones were cast down, and the Ancient of days did sit, whose garment was white as snow, and the hair of his head like the pure wool: his throne was like the fiery flame, and his wheels as burning fire.	And the Father himself, which hath sent me, hath borne witness of me. Ye have neither heard his voice at any time, nor seen his shape.	For the righteous LORD loveth righteousness; his countenance doth behold the upright.

The Eyes of God	The Mind of God	The Face of God
Revelation 19:12	Jeremiah 19:5	Deuteronomy 34:10
His eyes *were* as a flame of fire, and on his head *were* many crowns; and he had a name written, that no man knew, but he himself.	They have built also the high places of Baal, to burn their sons with fire for burnt offerings unto Baal, which I commanded not, nor spake it, neither came it into my mind.	And there arose not a prophet since in Israel like unto Moses, whom the LORD knew face to face.

The Ears of God	The Hands of God	The Fingers of God
Psalm 34:15	Hebrews 1:10	Exodus 31:18
The eyes of the LORD *are* upon the righteous, and his ears *are open* unto their cry.	And, Thou, Lord, in the beginning hast laid the foundation of the earth; and the heavens are the works of thine hands.	And he gave unto Moses, when he had made an end of communing with him upon mount Sinai, two tables of testimony, tables of stone, written with the finger of God.

The Arms of God	The Feet of God	The Mouth of God
John 12:38	1 Corinthians 15:27	Isaiah 1:20
That the saying of Esaias the prophet might be fulfilled, which he spake, Lord, who hath believed our report? And to whom hath the arm of the Lord been revealed?	For he hath put all things under his feet. But when he saith, all things are put under him, it is manifest that he is excepted, which did put all things under him.	But if ye refuse and rebel, ye shall be devoured with the sword: for the mouth of the LORD hath spoken it.

Of course, there are other scriptures that describe the characteristics of God, but please note that His characteristics are all symbolism used to represent His character.

FROM SALVATION TO ESCHATOLOGY

The journey of the human soul is an interesting one. It is a journey shrouded in mystery! It is a topic that is and will continue to be the subject of many religious debates. As a matter of fact, the subject of salvation versus damnation is such a sensitive one that it has completely divided believers, causing the emergence of many religions, false religions, denominations, and sects. And get this—the development of many of these faiths are not the result of an individual who simply misinterpreted the scriptures; all too often, sects and false religions are developed by men and women who absolutely refuse to accept the truth! In other words, they personally decided to create a truth that was more palatable for themselves!

Creation	Damnation	Salvation
Genesis 1:26-27	Genesis 3:17-19	Romans 10:9

There are three kingdoms.

Kingdom of Darkness	Kingdom of Man	Kingdom of God
Colossians 1:13	Daniel 4:17	Matthew 6:33

Like the journey from creation to salvation, the three kingdoms can be compared to the Israelites' plight and ultimate deliverance from Egypt.

Egypt	Wilderness	Promised Land
Exodus 1:11	Exodus 15:22	Joshua 21:43

First and foremost, what exactly is salvation? The Greek word for "salvation" is "sótéria," and it literally means "deliverance."

Salvation
c. 1200, originally in the Christian sense, "the saving of the soul," from Old French salvaciun and directly from Late Latin salvationem (nominative salvatio, a Church Latin translation of Greek soteria), noun of action from past-participle stem of salvare "to save" (see save (v.)). In general (non-religious) sense, attested from late 14c. Meaning "source of salvation" is from late 14c. Salvation Army is from 1878, founded by the Rev. William Booth.
Source: Online Etymology Dictionary

Save
c. 1200, "to deliver from some danger; rescue from peril, bring to safety," also "prevent the death of;" also theological, "to deliver from sin or its consequences; admit to eternal life; gain salvation," from Old French sauver "keep (safe), protect, redeem," from Late Latin salvare "make safe, secure," from Latin salvus "safe" (from PIE root *sol- "whole, well-kept"). From c. 1300 as "reserve for future use, hold back, store up instead of spending;" hence "keep possession of" (late 14c.).
Source: Online Etymology Dictionary

Deliverance
c. 1200, originally in the Christian sense, "the saving of the soul," from Old French salvaciun and directly from Late Latin salvationem (nominative salvatio, a Church Latin translation of Greek soteria), noun of action from past-participle stem of salvare "to save" (see save (v.)). In general (non-religious) sense, attested from late 14c. Meaning "source of salvation" is from late 14c. Salvation Army is from 1878, founded by the Rev. William Booth. c. 1300, deliveraunce, "action of setting free" in physical or spiritual senses, from Old French delivrance (12c., Modern French délivrance), from delivrer "to set free" (see deliver). Formerly also with senses now restricted to delivery: "childbirth; act of giving or transferring to another; utterance."
Source: Online Etymology Dictionary

Damnation

But what exactly are we being saved from? To answer this question, we have to look at a few scriptures.

Ezekiel 28:15-19	Revelation 12:7-9	Matthew 25:41
Thou wast perfect in thy ways from the day that thou wast created, till iniquity was found in thee. By the multitude of thy merchandise they have filled the midst of thee with violence, and thou hast	And there was war in heaven: Michael and his angels fought against the dragon; and the dragon fought and his angels, And prevailed not; neither was their place found any more in heaven. And the great dragon was cast out, that old serpent,	Then shall he say also unto them on the left hand, Depart from me, ye cursed, into everlasting fire, prepared for the devil and his angels,

sinned: therefore I will cast thee as profane out of the mountain of God: and I will destroy thee, O covering cherub, from the midst of the stones of fire. Thine heart was lifted up because of thy beauty, thou hast corrupted thy wisdom by reason of thy brightness: I will cast thee to the ground, I will lay thee before kings, that they may behold thee. Thou hast defiled thy sanctuaries by the multitude of thine iniquities, by the iniquity of thy traffick; therefore will I bring forth a fire from the midst of thee, it shall devour thee, and I will bring thee to ashes upon the earth in the sight of all them that behold thee. All they that know thee among the people shall be astonished at thee: thou shalt be a terror, and never shalt thou be any more.	called the Devil, and Satan, which deceiveth the whole world: he was cast out into the earth, and his angels were cast out with him.	

God created the Heavens and the Earth. There are three Heavens; they are:

First Heaven	Second Heaven	Third Heaven
Atmosphere Above Earth	Sun, Moon and Stars	God's Abode
Psalm 2:4	Genesis 1:16-17	Genesis 1:20

When Lucifer rebelled against God, he was cast into the Earth, along with his angels; this is why Satan is referred to as the prince of the power of the air. The angels of God reside in the

Second Heaven. Once Satan and his angels were cast into the Earth, the book of Revelation tells us that Satan went to make war with the "woman's seed." Revelation 12:13-17 reads, "And when the dragon saw that he was cast unto the earth, he persecuted the woman which brought forth the man child. And to the woman were given two wings of a great eagle, that she might fly into the wilderness, into her place, where she is nourished for a time, and times, and half a time, from the face of the serpent. And the serpent cast out of his mouth water as a flood after the woman, that he might cause her to be carried away of the flood. And the earth helped the woman, and the earth opened her mouth, and swallowed up the flood which the dragon cast out of his mouth. And the dragon was wroth with the woman, and went to make war with the remnant of her seed, which keeps the commandments of God, and have the testimony of Jesus Christ." Now, this story is a picture of two events. First, Satan waged war against mankind when he approached Eve in the Garden of Eden and began to deceive her. Why was he after the woman? Because she has a womb! This means that she has the ability to bring life into the Earth. Satan was (and is) terrified of God's decree regarding him and his angels, and he will stop at nothing to delay this word from coming to pass. So, he went after Adam's helpmate. The woman being given two wings to fly into the wilderness was a picture of mankind's descent from Eden. Within Eden is the garden that Adam and Eve were charged with maintaining, but outside of Eden is a wilderness. A garden is a place of order; a wilderness is a place of disorder. This is where we are right now! As believers, we are in the wilderness; we are currently caught up between Heaven and Earth. This is why the Bible says that we are in the world, but not of it. We live in the Earth realm, but we are citizens of God's Kingdom. But what about unbelievers? What does it mean to be damned?

When God pronounced judgment on Satan and his angels, His Word went forth, and because it is impossible for God to lie, when mankind fell, he fell under God's already declared Word. God could not take back what He'd decreed. He'd already created a place for Satan and his angels, but when mankind sinned, he fell under the law that had been established by God regarding spirits that rebelled against Him! What are we? Spirits living inside bodies, of course! Because God loves us and because He did not create Hell for mankind, He decided to create another decree; this decree would serve as a bridge or a get-out-of-Hell-free card. This decree is called Jesus Christ; this is why He is referred to as the Living Word of God! But in order for us to take hold of God's promise, we would have to use our will. We would have to accept Jesus Christ as our Lord and Savior, and He, in turn, would bare our sins in His own body; this allowed us to receive His righteousness (through faith) while He endured the punishment for our sins. Nevertheless, because He is and was sinless, Hell could not stake claim to Him, so the three days that He spent in Hell was time He used to set many of the people who had been locked up in Abraham's bosom free.

So what then is damnation? Damnation is a legal term that comes from the word "condemnation," which, of course, comes from the word "condemn." The word "condemn," means "to judge" or "to pronounce guilty." Damnation is the sentence imposed on those who have been declared guilty. Consider eternal damnation; it simply means that there is no end to a sentence. Who is YAHWEH? He is Alpha (the Beginning) and Omega (the End). He is eternal; there is no end to Him. He doesn't have a beginning; He is the Beginning! And it is for this reason that everything God creates is eternal, however, to limit or place restrictions on the space and duration of a thing, an event, or a creature, God created a mechanism called time. Darkness existed, and God spoke to the darkness, saying, "Let there be light." The book of Genesis then tells us that He separated the light from the darkness; He then called the light "day" and He called the darkness "night." This event was designed to place a limitation on darkness and create a space for light to dwell. Who is God? 1 John 1:5 reads, "This then is the message which we have heard of him, and declare unto you, that God is light, and in him is no darkness at all." Therefore, eternal damnation means to be sentenced to a place that is not subjected to time. Earth is subject to time, but Hell is not.

The Sentence

We understand that Satan and his angels were sentenced to eternal damnation, but what exactly would be their punishment? They would be cast into a fiery furnace that had been prepared by God for them. Nevertheless, despite what we've been taught, Hell and the lake of fire are not one and the same. How do we know this? Revelation 20:14 states, "And death and Hell were cast into the lake of fire. This is the second death." This scripture makes a distinction between Hell and the lake of fire.

The word "Hell" is a transliteration of the word "Sheol," which refers to the abode of the dead; another word for Sheol is "grave." It is also referred to as the "pit." In the New Testament, the word "Sheol" was replaced with the word "Hades." Let's look at the story of Korah. You can read the story in its entirety in Numbers 16, but below, you'll find a few snippets of the incident.

Numbers 16:1-7
Now Korah, the son of Izhar, the son of Kohath, the son of Levi, and Dathan and Abiram, the sons of Eliab, and On, the son of Peleth, sons of Reuben, took men: And they rose up before Moses, with certain of the children of Israel, two hundred and fifty princes of the assembly, famous in the congregation, men of renown: And they gathered themselves together against Moses and against Aaron, and said unto them, Ye take too much upon you, seeing all the congregation are holy, every one of them, and the LORD is among them: wherefore then lift

> ye up yourselves above the congregation of the LORD? And when Moses heard it, he fell upon his face: And he spake unto Korah and unto all his company, saying, Even to morrow the LORD will shew who are his, and who is holy; and will cause him to come near unto him: even him whom he hath chosen will he cause to come near unto him. This do; Take you censers, Korah, and all his company; And put fire therein, and put incense in them before the LORD to morrow: and it shall be that the man whom the LORD doth choose, he shall be holy: ye take too much upon you, ye sons of Levi.

Numbers 16:23-33

And the LORD spake unto Moses, saying, Speak unto the congregation, saying, Get you up from about the tabernacle of Korah, Dathan, and Abiram.
And Moses rose up and went unto Dathan and Abiram; and the elders of Israel followed him.
And he spake unto the congregation, saying, Depart, I pray you, from the tents of these wicked men, and touch nothing of theirs, lest ye be consumed in all their sins. So they gat up from the tabernacle of Korah, Dathan, and Abiram, on every side: and Dathan and Abiram came out, and stood in the door of their tents, and their wives, and their sons, and their little children. And Moses said, Hereby ye shall know that the LORD hath sent me to do all these works; for I have not done them of mine own mind. If these men die the common death of all men, or if they be visited after the visitation of all men; then the LORD hath not sent me. But if the LORD make a new thing, and the earth open her mouth, and swallow them up, with all that appertain unto them, and they go down quick into the pit; then ye shall understand that these men have provoked the LORD.
And it came to pass, as he had made an end of speaking all these words, that the ground clave asunder that was under them: And the earth opened her mouth, and swallowed them up, and their houses, and all the men that appertained unto Korah, and all their goods. They, and all that appertained to them, went down alive into the pit, and the earth closed upon them: and they perished from among the congregation.

The pit referenced in the aforementioned story is the infamous Sheol. Again, this is the space under the earth referred to as the grave. However, the pit is for the dead, but the lake of fire was created for Satan and his angels, and their sentence in the lake of fire is eternal. Why? Because spirits are eternal.

The word "Hell" was first mentioned in Matthew 5:22. Here, Jesus goes on record saying, "But I say unto you, That whosoever is angry with his brother without a cause shall be in danger of the judgment: and whosoever shall say to his brother, Raca, shall be in danger of the council:

but whosoever shall say, Thou fool, shall be in danger of Hell fire." In this particular verse of scripture, the word "Hell" comes from the Greek word "Gehenna." Gehenna was a place outside of Jerusalem where the Israelites went to burn their trash; there, the fire never went out. But wait a minute! The Bible tells us that Death and Hell will be tossed into the lake of fire. How then is there fire already in Hell? After all, the Bible describes Hell as being a place where people will experience:

- weeping
- the gnashing of teeth

The First and the Second Death

There are two deaths that the Bible speaks of. They are the first death and the second death. What exactly is death from a biblical standpoint? The Greek word for "death" is "thanatos." Let's examine this word a little closer.

Thanatos
1) the death of the body
1a) that separation (whether natural or violent) of the soul and the body by which the life on earth is ended
1b) with the implied idea of future misery in Hell
1b1) the power of death
1c) since the nether world, the abode of the dead, was conceived as being very dark, it is equivalent to the region of thickest darkness, i.e. figuratively, a region enveloped in the darkness of ignorance and sin
2) metaphorically, the loss of that life which alone is worthy of the name
2a) the misery of the soul arising from sin, which begins on earth but lasts and increases after the death of the body in Hell
3) the miserable state of the wicked dead in Hell
4) in the widest sense, death comprising all the miseries arising from sin, as well physical death as the loss of a life consecrated to God and blessed in him on earth, to be followed by wretchedness in Hell
Part of Speech: noun masculine
Relation: from G2348
Source: Thayer's Greek Lexicon

First Death	Second Death
Physical	Spiritual
The separation of man's spirit from his body; the expulsion of man's spirit from the realm of the Earth.	The permanent and final separation from man's spirit from God's Spirit; eternal damnation.
Genesis 3:19	Revelation 20:14

More Facts About Biblical Deaths

- The first man to die was Abel who, of course, was murdered by his brother, Cain.
- Adam lived to be 930 years old before he tasted death.
- Living a whopping 969 years, Methuselah was the longest-living human on Earth.
- The first person to ever be revived from death was the son of the widow of Zarephath by the prophet Elijah.
- The first person to ever be resurrected or raised from the dead is Jesus Christ.
- Revival and resurrection are not the same! To be revived indicates that the person is revived through prayer. To be resurrected means to be restored to life by God's Spirit.

Ten People in the Bible Who Were Raised from the Dead	
The Widow of Zarepheth's Son (1 Kings 17:17-24)	Shunammite Woman's Son (2 Kings 4:18-37)
Unnamed Israelite Man (2 Kings 13:20-21)	Widow of Nain's Son (Luke 7:11-17)
Jairus' Daughter (Luke 8:49-56)	Lazarus (John 11:1-44)
Jesus Christ (Matthew 28:1-20)	Many Saints Who'd Died Before Jesus (Matthew 27:50-54)
Tabitha (Dorcas in Greek) (Acts 9:36-42)	Eutychus (Acts 20:7-12)

Note: this list does not include the many men and women who were raised from the dead by Jesus and His disciples.

The Creation of Mankind

Genesis 1:26-28 reads, "And God said, Let us make man in our image, after our likeness: and let them have dominion over the fish of the sea, and over the fowl of the air, and over the cattle, and over all the earth, and over every creeping thing that creepeth upon the earth. So God created man in his own image, in the image of God created he him; male and female created he them. And God blessed them, and God said unto them, Be fruitful, and multiply, and replenish the earth, and subdue it: and have dominion over the fish of the sea, and over the fowl of the air, and over every living thing that moveth upon the earth." Genesis 2:4-7 seems to depict a very separate but similar event; it reads, "These are the generations of the heavens and of the earth when they were created, in the day that the LORD God made the earth and the heavens, and every plant of the field before it was in the earth, and every herb of the field before it grew: for the LORD God had not caused it to rain upon the earth, and there was not a man to till the ground. But there went up a mist from the earth, and watered the whole face of the ground. And the LORD God formed man of the dust of the ground, and breathed into his nostrils the breath of life; and man became a living soul." Many theologians have debated as to whether or not Adam and Eve were the first humans to live on the Earth, and they use these two scriptures as the basis for their theories. But while they appear to depict two events, the truth is, God created the spirit of mankind before He created our bodies! The event in Genesis 1 details the creation of Adam and Eve's spirits, but Genesis 2 details the creation of Adam's body, from which God would eventually pull Eve's body. Why is this important to note? Because they were initially spirits; they'd been created and given instructions, but in order for them to carry out these instructions in a natural environment, they needed earth suits or, better yet, bodies! This was similar to the manner in which God created the Earth. First, He created the Heavens and the Earth, but according to Genesis, the Earth was without form and void. Without form, meaning, it had no physical matter; void, meaning, it had no light, life or revelation! In other words, God created the Heavens and the Earth within Himself; it was but an idea, howbeit, externally, it had not materialized. That is, until God spoke to it. How did He respond? He said, "Let there be light." Again, this is similar to how God created mankind. First, He created the blueprint for mankind in His mind; then He gave life to His idea by speaking to it. Adam and Eve came into existence, but their bodies were without form (they hadn't been formed yet) and void (absent of revelation or instructions). God then formed Adam's body and breathed the breath of life into him. He then dealt with the void by giving Adam an assignment. Hear me—our assignments are our identities; this is the very purpose for which we were born! This isn't necessarily a job; the work we do is designed to complete a specific goal. Adam's job was to till the Garden of Eden, but what Adam didn't know was that soil, in the Bible, is used to represent flesh, meaning, Adam's job was to cultivate his flesh until he became more like God! So, God dealt with the void by:

1. Giving Adam and Eve an assignment (Genesis 1:28, Genesis 2:15).

2. Positioning Adam by placing him in the Garden of Eden (Genesis 2:8).
3. Setting boundaries in Adam's life (Genesis 2:16).
4. Giving Adam a test (Genesis 2:19).
5. Giving Adam a help meet (Genesis 2:21-22).

The Death of Man, the Emergence of Mankind

When Adam and Eve sinned, they paved the way for Death to come and collect their bodies. This would once again separate them from their flesh, which would then render them powerless in a natural setting. Because of this, their spirits had to go to a spiritual place; they could not remain in the realm of the Earth. Howbeit, because sin separated man from God, they could not return to Him initially. There was no other place for them but Hell; this was the pit or the temporary place of punishment for Satan and his angels. The eternal place for Satan and his crew is the lake of fire. Let's look at some scriptural evidence.

Revelation 20:1-3
And I saw an angel come down from heaven, having the key of the bottomless pit and a great chain in his hand. And he laid hold on the dragon, that old serpent, which is the Devil, and Satan, and bound him a thousand years, And cast him into the bottomless pit, and shut him up, and set a seal upon him, that he should deceive the nations no more, till the thousand years should be fulfilled: and after that he must be loosed a little season.

Revelation 20:7-10
And when the thousand years are expired, Satan shall be loosed out of his prison, And shall go out to deceive the nations which are in the four quarters of the earth, Gog and Magog, to gather them together to battle: the number of whom is as the sand of the sea. And they went up on the breadth of the earth, and compassed the camp of the saints about, and the beloved city: and fire came down from God out of heaven, and devoured them. And the devil that deceived them was cast into the lake of fire and brimstone, where the beast and the false prophet are, and shall be tormented day and night for ever and ever.

Jude 1:6 confirms this; it reads, "And the angels which kept not their first estate, but left their own habitation, he hath reserved in everlasting chains under darkness unto the judgment of the great day." In other translations, the word "unto" is replaced with "until," indicating that this pit or place of darkness is a temporary abode, however, the final destination for Satan, his angels and those who are not found in the Lamb's Book of Life is the lake of fire that burns for eternity.

Revelation 20:11-15
And I saw a great white throne, and him that sat on it, from whose face the earth and the heaven fled away; and there was found no place for them. And I saw the dead, small and great, stand before God; and the books were opened: and another book was opened, which is the book of life: and the dead were judged out of those things which were written in the books, according to their works. And the sea gave up the dead which were in it; and death and Hell delivered up the dead which were in them: and they were judged every man according to their works. And death and Hell were cast into the lake of fire. This is the second death. And whosoever was not found written in the book of life was cast into the lake of fire.

To die meant that Adam and Eve would ultimately be separated from their earth-suits or, better yet, their bodies. A man's body is what legalizes his existence in the Earth because the Earth is a natural place. Spirits, on the other hand, have their own domain. This means that a spirit that had been separated from his or her body could not wander around in the Earth; this is why Apostle Paul said, "We are confident, I say, and willing rather to be absent from the body, and to be present with the Lord," indicating the final fate of the believer. Unbelievers, on the other hand, had no place found for them in Heaven, just as there was no place for Satan or his angels in Heaven.

To better understand death, consider these facts:
- God is Light (Life), but not in the context by which we understand light (see 1 John 1:5, John 1:4).
- Two cannot walk together except they are in agreement (see Amos 3:3).
- When mankind sinned, he fell out of agreement with God, meaning he could no longer walk with God. Consequently, God (Life) separated Himself from mankind. This is the very picture of what it means to die.
- Adam and Eve didn't immediately give up their ghosts. Think of a cellphone. You can plug it in and charge it up, but once you remove it from the charger, it then begins to power down. It may retain a charge for one to a few days, but eventually, it will die (power down). Thankfully, it can be revived if it is plugged into a power source once again.

Originally, Adam and Eve were referred to as "man," but after their fall, they were referred to as "mankind," meaning, they became a kind of man; this is why God started referring to them as mankind. Another word for mankind is human; the word "human" means "humbled man" or "humiliated man." It means lower than a man. In other words, we became a generic form of what God originally created us to be.

Genesis	Gene	Genetic	Generation	Generational	Generic

It all started in Genesis. Genesis is not just a chapter in the Bible, the word "genesis" means beginning, source and origin. Who is God again? He is Alpha (the Beginning) and Omega (the End). He is also Abba. The word "Abba" means "father," and the word "father" means "originator" and "source." Hear me—we originated in Genesis! Genesis is not a what, it's a who! Who is Genesis? The Beginning! This is where we get the word "gene," which, according to Oxford Languages means "a unit of heredity which is transferred from a parent to offspring and is held to determine some characteristic of the offspring." Remember, we were made "in" the image and likeness of God (see Genesis 1:27); we are little gods (see Psalm 82:6). We come complete with:

1. A spirit: (breath, wind).
2. Will: the ability to think and do as we choose.
3. Dominion: a measure of the rule.

Nevertheless, when our genes were perverted, we became generic; we became mankind. Get this—man is the heir to the Kingdom of God and all that comes with it, but mankind isn't. This is why Jesus referred to Himself as "Son of Man" and not "Son of Mankind." When we accept Jesus as our Lord and Savior, we position ourselves to be heirs of the Kingdom—we position ourselves to mature into what and who God originally designed us to be.

Galatians 4:1-7
Now I say, That the heir, as long as he is a child, differeth nothing from a servant, **though he be lord of all**; but is under tutors and governors until the time appointed of the father. Even so we, when we were children, were in bondage under the elements of the world: But when the fullness of the time was come, God sent forth his Son, made of a woman, made under the law, To redeem them that were under the law, **that we might receive the adoption of sons**. And **because** ye are sons, God hath sent forth the Spirit of his Son into your hearts, crying, Abba, Father. Wherefore thou art no more a servant, but a son; and if a son, then an heir of God through Christ.

ESCHAT**OLOGY**

"the part of theology concerned with death, judgment, and the final destiny of the soul and of humankind" (Oxford Languages).

UNDERSTANDING ESCHATOLOGY

Acts 2:17: And it shall come to pass in the **last days**, saith God, I will pour out of my Spirit upon all flesh: and your sons and your daughters shall prophesy, and your young men shall see visions, and your old men shall dream dreams.

(eschatos + logos = the "last word")

Eschatology
1834, from Latinized form of Greek eskhatos "last, furthest, uttermost, extreme, most remote" in time, space, degree (from PIE *eghs-ko-, suffixed form of *eghs "out;" see ex-) + -ology. In theology, the study of the four last things (death, judgment, heaven, Hell). Related: Eschatological; eschatologically.
Source: Online Etymology Dictionary

Eschatology
Eschatology, the doctrine of the last things. It was originally a Western term, referring to Jewish, Christian, and Muslim beliefs about the end of history, the resurrection of the dead, the Last Judgment, the messianic era, and the problem of theodicy (the vindication of God's justice). Historians of religion have applied the term to similar themes and concepts in the religions of nonliterate peoples, ancient Mediterranean and Middle Eastern cultures, and Eastern civilizations. Eschatological archetypes also can be found in various secular liberation movements.
Source: Encyclopedia Britannica

Eschatology is the study of end times or last things. It comes from the Greek word "eschaton" (also eschatos), which literally means "last." It is the study of the end and the events that lead to it. There are three views or doctrines regarding eschatology; they are:

Premillennialism	Postmillennialism	Amillennialism

Revelation 20:1-7: And I saw an angel come down from heaven, having the key of the bottomless pit and a great chain in his hand. And he laid hold on the dragon, that old serpent, which is the Devil, and Satan, and bound him a thousand years, and cast him into the bottomless pit, and shut him up, and set a seal upon him, that he should deceive the nations no more, till the thousand years should be fulfilled: and after that he must be loosed a little season. And I saw thrones, and they sat upon them, and judgment was given unto them: and I saw the

souls of them that were beheaded for the witness of Jesus, and for the word of God, and which had not worshipped the beast, neither his image, neither had received his mark upon their foreheads, or in their hands; and they lived and reigned with Christ a thousand years. But the rest of the dead lived not again until the thousand years were finished. This is the first resurrection. Blessed and holy is he that hath part in the first resurrection: on such the second death hath no power, but they shall be priests of God and of Christ, and shall reign with him a thousand years.

Milliennium
A thousand years; the name given to the era mentioned in Revelation 20:1-7. Some maintain that Christ will personally appear on earth for the purpose of establishing his kingdom at the beginning of this millennium. Those holding this view are usually called "millenarians." On the other hand, it is maintained, more in accordance with the teaching of Scripture, we think, that Christ's second advent will not be premillennial, and that the right conception of the prospects and destiny of his kingdom is that which is taught, e.g., in the parables of the leaven and the mustard-seed. The triumph of the gospel, it is held, must be looked for by the wider and more efficient operation of the very forces that are now at work in extending the gospel; and that Christ will only come again at the close of this dispensation to judge the world at the "last day." The millennium will thus precede his coming.
Source: Easton's Bible Dictionary

Premillennialism
(among some Christian Protestants) the doctrine that the prophesied millennium of blessedness will begin with the imminent Second Coming of Christ.
Source: Oxford Languages

Premillennialism is a dominant theory or doctrine that states that the events foretold in the book of Revelations are both futuristic and literal. These events include:

The Rapture	The Second Coming of Christ
The Resurrection of the Dead	The Final Judgment

Supporters of the doctrine or theory of Premillennialism are divided into two categories or sects:
- **Historic Premillennialism**

Understanding Eschatology

- **Dispensational Premillennialism**

Historic (Covenant) Premillennialism	Dispensational Premillennialism
Supporters of this theory argue that the rapture of the church will follow after the Great Tribulation, as foretold in Daniel 12:1-3. Adherents of this view state that the church will meet Jesus in the air upon His return and will aid Him in His one-thousand year rule on the Earth. Supporters of Historic Premillennialism say that the millennium will be for God's bride (the Church), not Israel.	Supporters of this theory argue that the rapture of the church will finalize or end the current stage of the church. Dispensatinalists also believe that the one-thousand year reign of Jesus, as predicted in Revelation 20:6, is a literal event that will take place, whereas, opposers of this theory believe that the mention of a thousand-year reign is simply figurative.

Postmillennialism

(among some Christian Protestants) the doctrine that the Second Coming of Christ will be the culmination of the prophesied millennium of blessedness.

Source: Oxford Languages

Postmillennialism supporters believe that Jesus' Second Coming will occur after the millennium. Postmillennialists don't believe that the thousand-year reign as foretold in Revelation 20:6 is the literal number of years that Jesus will reign; instead, supporters of postmillennialism assert that the mention of one-thousand years in the biblical text simply means "a long time," and that Christ will return after Christians have established God's Kingdom on Earth. Postmillenialists ascribe to the belief that the entire world will eventually become Christian, and it is then and only then that the Christ will return, The problem with this theory, however, is that the Bible prophesies that the last days will be "terrible times."

Amillennialism

the view in Christian eschatology which states that Christ is presently reigning through the Church, and that the "1000 years" of Revelation 20:1-6 is a metaphorical reference to the present church age which will culminate in Christ's return.

Source: Theopedia

"A" millennialism literally means "no" millennium. Supporters of this view, like postmillenialists, do not believe that there will be a literal one-thousand year reign of Jesus Christ. Post millennialists do not believe that there will be a one-thousand year rule of Christ. They believe that Christ is now reigning from the throne of David and that Christ is ruling over this current stage of the church. It goes without saying that Christ is currently ruling, however, amillenialists state that the biblical prophecy of a thousand-year rule is simply referencing the state or stage that the church is currently in.

Four Approaches to Eschatology

Futurist	Preterist
Historicist	Idealist

Futurist

The Futurist approach treats the Book of Revelation mostly as unfulfilled prophecy taking place in some yet undetermined future.

Source: Wikipedia

Preterist

The Preterist approach interprets Revelation chiefly as having had prophetic fulfillment in the past, principally in the events of the first century CE.

Source: Wikipedia

Historicist

The Historicist approach places Revelation within the context of history, identifying figures and passages in Revelation with major historical people and events. This view was commonly held by the early Christian church, then among the predecessors to Protestantism, such as John Wycliffe, and later by the majority of Protestant Reformers, such as Martin Luther, John Calvin, and John Wesley. Further supporters of this view included Isaac Newton (1642-1727), among others.

Source: Wikipedia

Idealist
The Idealist approach sees the events of Revelation as neither past nor future actualities, but as purely symbolic accounts, dealing with the ongoing struggle and ultimate triumph of good over evil.
Source: Wikipedia

Hell, Hades, Sheol, Gehenna, the Abyss and the Lake of Fire

One of the most divided and seemingly complex topics in Christian theology is Hell or, better yet, the holding place for the unregenerate. As we discovered earlier, the words Sheol and Hell are synonymous; they literally mean "the abode for the dead" or the "grave." In the New Testament, the word "Sheol" was replaced with "Hades," however, some theologians suggest that both Sheol and Hades are compartments of Hell. But before we dive deeper into this topic, what exactly is Hell? In short, Hell is the toxic waste system of the spiritual world. Remember, God created the Heavens and the Earth, but when Lucifer was demoted to Satan and his angels were demoted to demons, there was no place found for them in Heaven anymore. What was God to do with them? After all, spirits are eternal beings. He couldn't just kill them because He'd given them eternal life, therefore, He had to place them somewhere! "And the great dragon was cast out, that old serpent, called the Devil, and Satan, which deceiveth the whole world: he was cast out into the earth, and his angels were cast out with him" (Revelation 12:9). But get this—Earth was not created for Satan and his angels, therefore, Earth served as a temporary holding place. This is similar to how we store waste in the United States. Where does trash go once you're done with it? It eventually finds itself in a landfill, but even in the landfill, because the trash is made up of matter, it's going to take up space. To free up this space, the trash has to be burned; right?! What other way can you break down matter? The same way we have to get rid of waste in the natural realm is the same way that waste has to be processed in the spiritual world. Get this—everything that God creates is eternal because He is eternal; this is why He created Hell. He had to create an eternal place to store and eradicate spirits that were contrary to His being! This is why Revelation 14:11 details the finality of those who received the mark of the beast (the unsaved or unregenerate); it reads, "And the smoke of their torment ascendeth up for ever and ever: and they have no rest day nor night, who worship the beast and his image, and whosoever receiveth the mark of his name." Again, Satan and his angels were temporarily placed in the Earth, but the Earth was created for man (not mankind). All the same, the Earth was not created for Satan and his angels. So, the Earth served (and still serves) as a landfill, but the ultimate destination for all fallen angels is the lake of fire.

Understanding Eschatology

Revelation 4:6 reads, "And before the throne there was a sea of glass like unto crystal: and in the midst of the throne, and round about the throne, were four beasts full of eyes before and behind." In Greek mythology, Hades, Sheol and the Abyss are all compartments of Hell. Hades is where the Greeks believed that the infamous fire resides. Sheol is believed to be a dark place that houses people who weren't necessarily good but weren't entirely bad either; they simply existed. The Abyss, on the other hand, is the place that they believe God throws all of the waste into. Amazingly enough, Egyptian mythology promotes the concept that there is a sea that separates the living from the dead. In this, the spiritual world is depicted as water. In an amazing book entitled "The Legend of the Jews," the author (Louis Ginzberg) said, "The firmament is not the same as the heavens of the first day. It is the crystal stretched forth over the heads of the Hayyot, from which the heavens derive their light, as the earth derives its light from the sun. This firmament saves the earth from being engulfed by the waters of the heavens; it forms the partition between the waters above and the waters below." This brings to mind two scriptures in the book of Genesis.

Genesis 1:1-4	Genesis 1:6-8
In the beginning God created the heaven and the earth. And the earth was without form, and void; and darkness was upon the face of the	And God said, Let there be a firmament in the midst of the waters, and let it divide the waters from the waters. And God made the

deep. And the Spirit of God moved upon the face of the waters. And God said, Let there be light: and there was light. And God saw the light, that it was good: and God divided the light from the darkness.	firmament, and divided the waters which were under the firmament from the waters which were above the firmament: and it was so. And God called the firmament Heaven. And the evening and the morning were the second day.

The waters above, according to Mr. Ginzberg are the floor of the spiritual world, but the waters above are the ceiling of our world. He goes on to say, "It was made to crystallize into the solid it is by the heavenly fire, which broke its bounds, and condensed the surface of the firmament. Thus fire made a division between the celestial and the terrestrial at the time of creation, as it did at the revelation on Mount Sinai. The firmament is not more than three fingers thick, nevertheless it divides two such heavy bodies as the waters below, which are the foundations for the nether world, and the waters above, which are the foundations for the seven heavens, the Divine Throne, and the abode of the angels." Hear me—in the beginning, God created the Heavens and the Earth. When we hear the word "Earth," we immediately think about our planet. Copernicus, Ptolemy and Galileo all thought that the Earth was at the center of the universe. We eventually discovered that this wasn't true, but when the Bible talks about Heaven and Earth, it's talking about two realms: the spiritual realm and the natural or material realm. It's not talking about the planet Earth. Where was this all created? Think of it this way. When a woman gets pregnant, where is her child created? In her womb; right?! And that child is surrounded by water. So, when God was pregnant with the idea of Earth, what was His idea surrounded by? The answer is obvious—water! Who is God? He is Alpha (the Beginning) and Omega (the End). This means that when the scripture says, "In the beginning, God created the Heavens and the Earth, the Author was not referencing time, He meant that God created the Heavens and the Earth inside of Himself! What are they looking for on every planet? Water, of course, because wherever there is water, there is life! In short, what this all means is, God created a space between the natural world and the spiritual world, and then He crystallized it with fire. According to Mr. Ginzberg, this sea or membrane is only three fingers thick, meaning, the gap between our world and the spiritual world is so thin that both worlds often collide.

Gehenna and the Abyss

Gehenna

This verse is the basis of the later Jewish conception of Gehenna as the place of everlasting punishment (see Salmond's "Christian Doctrine of Immortality"). Gehenna is the Hebrew Ge-Hinnom (Valley of Hinnom), the place where, of old, human sacrifices were offered to Moloch,

Understanding Eschatology

and for this reason desecrated by King Josiah (2 Kings 23:10). Afterwards it became a receptacle for filth and refuse, and Rabbinical tradition asserts that it was the custom to cast out unclean corpses there, to be burned or to undergo decomposition. This is, in all probability, the scene which had imprinted itself on the imagination of the writer, and which was afterwards projected into the unseen world as an image of endless retribution. The Talmudic theology locates the mouth of hell in the Valley of Hinnom.

Source: Biblehub/Professor J. Skinner, D.D.

2 Kings 23:9-10	Isaiah 66:23-24
Nevertheless the priests of the high places came not up to the altar of the LORD in Jerusalem, but they did eat of the unleavened bread among their brethren. And he defiled Topheth, which is in the valley of the children of Hinnom, that no man might make his son or his daughter to pass through the fire to Molech.	And it shall come to pass, that from one new moon to another, and from one sabbath to another, shall all flesh come to worship before me, saith the LORD. And they shall go forth, and look upon the carcases of the men that have transgressed against me: for their worm shall not die, neither shall their fire be quenched; and they shall be an abhorring unto all flesh.

Abyss

Figuratively, "unfathomable," "boundless." "Abyss" does not occur in the King James Version but the Revised Version (British and American) so transliterates abussos in each case. The King James Version renders the Greek by "the deep" in two passages (Luke 8:31 Romans 10:7). In Revelation the King James Version renders by "the bottomless pit" (Revelation 9:1, 2, 11; Revelation 11:7; Revelation 17:8; 20:1, 3). In the Septuagint abussos is the rendering of the Hebrew word tehom. According to primitive Semitic cosmogony the earth was supposed to rest on a vast body of water which was the source of all springs of water and rivers (Genesis 1:2 Deuteronomy 8:7 Psalm 24:2; Psalm 136:6). This subterranean ocean is sometimes described as "the water under the earth" (Exodus 20:4 Deuteronomy 5:8). According to Job 41:32 tehom is the home of the leviathan in which he plows his hoary path of foam. The Septuagint never uses abussos as a rendering of sheol (= Sheol = Hades) and probably tehom never meant the "abode of the dead" which was the ordinary meaning of Sheol. In Psalm 71:20 tehom is used figuratively, and denotes "many and sore troubles" through which the psalmist has passed (compare Jonah 2:5). But in the New Testament the word abussos means the "abode of demons." In Luke 8:31 the King James Version renders "into the deep" (Weymouth and The Twentieth Century New Testament = "into the bottomless pit"). The demons do not wish to be sent to their place of punishment before their destined time. Mark simply says "out of the country" (Luke 5:10). In Romans 10:7 the word is equivalent to Hades, the abode of the dead. In Revelation (where the King James Version renders invariably "the bottomless pit") abussos denotes the abode of evil spirits, but not the place of final punishment; it is therefore to be distinguished from the "lake of fire and brimstone" where the beast and the false prophet are, and into which the Devil is to be finally cast (Revelation 19:20; Revelation 20:10).

Source: International Standard Bible Encyclopedia

2 Peter 2:4	Romans 10:6-7
For if God spared not the angels that sinned, but cast them down to hell, and delivered them into chains of darkness, to be reserved unto judgment.	But the righteousness which is of faith speaketh in this manner: "Say not in thine heart, 'Who shall ascend into Heaven?'" (that is, to bring Christ down from above) or, "'Who shall descend into the deep?'" (that is, to bring up Christ again from the dead).

The angels mentioned in 2 Peter 2:4 are believed to be the angels who came to Earth to sleep with human women. Genesis 6:1-2 details this event; it reads, "And it came to pass, when men began to multiply on the face of the earth, and daughters were born unto them, that the sons of God saw the daughters of men that they were fair; and they took them wives of all which they chose." When the scripture says that these angels were cast into Hell, the word "Hell" is likely the same as Gehenna. Notice that the scripture says that they are to be reserved there until Judgment, meaning, Gehenna is a temporary holding place for spirits. This is similar to Gehenna, the former landfill used by the Israelites. Ultimately, the trash stored there would be burned. What is going to happen to Satan and his angels? "And the devil that deceived them was cast into the lake of fire and brimstone, where the beast and the false prophet are, and shall be tormented day and night for ever and ever" (Revelation 20:10).

Revelation 20:1-3
And I saw an angel come down from heaven, having the key of the bottomless pit and a great chain in his hand. And he laid hold on the dragon, that old serpent, which is the Devil, and Satan, and bound him a thousand years, and cast him into the bottomless pit, and shut him up, and set a seal upon him, that he should deceive the nations no more, till the thousand years should be fulfilled: and after that he must be loosed a little season.

Note: Another word for "bottomless pit" is "abyss." Notice that the pit has no bottom; this isn't in reference to a solid structure, considering that this scripture is talking about the spiritual realm. The word "bottomless" here means that it has no end. Time is not an element in the spirit world, so the word "bottomless" simply refers to eternity. Note: Eternity is not a chronos concept; eternity has no end or beginning; it simply is (meaning, it simply exists).

Revelation 20:7-10
And when the thousand years are expired, Satan shall be loosed out of his prison, and shall go out to deceive the nations which are in the four quarters of the earth, Gog and Magog, to gather them together to battle: the number of whom is as the sand of the sea. and they went up on the breadth of the earth, and compassed the camp of the saints about, and the beloved city: and fire came down from God out of heaven, and devoured them. And the devil that deceived them was cast into the lake of fire and brimstone, where the beast and the false prophet are, and shall be tormented day and night for ever and ever.

The prison mentioned here, once again, is the Abyss. What's the difference between the Abyss and Gehenna? There is much debate surrounding these two, and many theologians believe that they are one and the same, but what we do know is that they are both temporary holding places; this doesn't mean that they are limited by space and time. It simply means that their existence will be eventually eradicated by the lake of fire.

Lake of Fire

Revelation 14:9-11
And the third angel followed them, saying with a loud voice, If any man worship the beast and his image, and receive his mark in his forehead, or in his hand, the same shall drink of the wine of the wrath of God, which is poured out without mixture into the cup of his indignation; and he shall be tormented with fire and brimstone in the presence of the holy angels, and in the presence of the Lamb: And the smoke of their torment ascendeth up for ever and ever: and they have no rest day nor night, who worship the beast and his image, and whosoever receiveth the mark of his name.

Remember, both Death and Hades will be thrown into the Lake of Fire. The Lake of Fire, in short, is God's wrath poured out without mixture, meaning, full strength or undiluted. Another way to say this is without grace and without mercy; the Lake of Fire represents the fullness of God's wrath without any constraints or restraints. Fire is used to symbolize God's judgment; we see this in a few stories depicting His use of fire to judge the wicked. Let's look at a few scriptures.

Genesis 19:24	2 Kings 1:12	Daniel 7:10
Then the LORD rained upon Sodom and upon Gomorrah brimstone and fire from the LORD out of heaven.	And Elijah answered and said unto them, If I be a man of God, let fire come down from heaven, and consume thee and thy fifty. And the fire of God came down from heaven, and consumed him and his fifty.	A fiery stream issued and came forth from before him: thousand thousands ministered unto him, and ten thousand times ten thousand stood before him: the judgment was set, and the books were opened.

Popup Memory Test

What is the difference between Hell, Hades, Sheol, Gehenna, the Abyss and the Lake of Fire? List as many differences as you can remember.

SOTERIOLOGY

"theology dealing with salvation especially as effected by Jesus Christ" (Merriam Webster).

Understanding Soteriology

John 3:16: For God so loved the world, that he gave his only Son, that whoever believes in him should not perish but have eternal life.

From Greek sōtēria 'salvation'+ -logy.

Soteriology
1847, in reference to health; 1864 in reference to salvation, from German soteriologie, from Greek soteria "preservation, salvation," from soizein "save, preserve," related to sōs "safe, healthy," which is of uncertain origin (perhaps from PIE root *teue- "to swell," on the notion of "to be strong"). With -ology.
Source: Online Etymology Dictionary

Soteriology
Soteriology (/səˌtɪəriˈɒlədʒi/; Greek: σωτηρία sōtēria "salvation" from σωτήρ sōtēr "savior, preserver" and λόγος logos "study" or "word" is the study of religious doctrines of salvation. Salvation theory occupies a place of special significance in many religions. In the academic field of religious studies, soteriology is understood by scholars as representing a key theme in a number of different religions and is often studied in a comparative context; that is, comparing various ideas about what salvation is and how it is obtained.
Source: Wikipedia

Soteriology, in short, is the branch of theology that deals with the doctrine of salvation. It comes from the Greek word "sótéria," which literally means "deliverance." It also comes from the Greek word "sozo," which can be translated as:
- To save from certain death.
- To be healed.
- To be made whole.
- To preserve.

Again, what do we need to be saved from?
- Enemies (Exodus 14:13)
- Slavery/Physical Bondage (Psalm 53:6)
- Our Sins (Romans 1:16, Philippians 2:12-13)

- Difficult Circumstances (Psalm 78:22)
- Sickness/Physical Illness (James 5:15)
- Storms (Matthew 8:25)
- Eternal Damnation (John 5:29)

Salvation	Save	Safe
c. 1200, originally in the Christian sense, "the saving of the soul," from Old French salvaciun and directly from Late Latin salvationem (nominative salvatio, a Church Latin translation of Greek soteria), noun of action from past-participle stem of salvare "to save". In general (non-religious) sense, attested from late 14c. Meaning "source of salvation" is from late 14c. Salvation Army is from 1878, founded by the Rev. William Booth.	c. 1200, "to deliver from some danger; rescue from peril, bring to safety," also "prevent the death of;" also theological, "to deliver from sin or its consequences; admit to eternal life; gain salvation," from Old French sauver "keep (safe), protect, redeem," from Late Latin salvare "make safe, secure," from Latin salvus "safe" (from PIE root *sol- "whole, well-kept"). From c. 1300 as "reserve for future use, hold back, store up instead of spending;" hence "keep possession of" (late 14c.). Save face (1898) first was used among the British community in China and is said to be from Chinese; it has not been found in Chinese, but tiu lien "to lose face" does occur. To not (do something) to save one's life is recorded from 1848. To save (one's) breath "cease talking or arguing" is from 1926.	c. 1300, "unscathed, unhurt, uninjured; free from danger or molestation, in safety, secure; saved spiritually, redeemed, not damned;" from Old French sauf "protected, watched-over; assured of salvation," from Latin salvus "uninjured, in good health, safe," related to salus "good health," saluber "healthful," all from PIE *solwos from root *sol- "whole, well-kept." As a quasi-preposition from c. 1300, on model of French and Latin cognates. From late 14c. as "rescued, delivered; protected; left alive, unkilled." Meaning "not exposed to danger" (of places) is attested from late 14c.; of actions, etc., "free from risk," first recorded 1580s. Meaning "sure, reliable, not a danger" is from c. 1600. Sense of "conservative, cautious" is from 1823. Paired alliteratively with sound (adj.) from late 14c. The noun safe-conduct (late 13c.) is from Old French sauf-conduit (13c.).

Source: Online Etymology Dictionary

Creation	Damnation	Salvation
The formation of man.	The great fall of mankind.	The deliverance of mankind.

Reminders:
- There was no place found in Heaven for Satan and his angels because they had transitioned from being spirits of Light (God) to dark (evil) spirits.
- God placed Adam and Eve in the Garden of Eden to till the ground, but when the couple fell, like Satan, there was no longer any place found for them in Eden because Eden was created for man, not mankind.
- Hell was created for Satan and his angels.
- Man fell under God's already declared Word once they fell into sin.
- God sent us a Redeemer (Jesus Christ) to save us from eternal damnation and restore us to eternal life with Him.

Outline of Bible Usage
I. deliverance, preservation, safety, salvation
(a)   deliverance from the molestation of enemies
(b)   in an ethical sense, that which concludes to the soul's safety or salvation
   i. of Messianic salvation
I. salvation as the present possession of all true Christians
II. future salvation, the sum of benefits and blessings which the Christians, redeemed from all earthly ills, will enjoy after the visible return of Christ from heaven in the consummated and eternal kingdom of God.

Source: Blue Letter Bible

BUT WHEN THE FULLNESS OF THE TIME WAS COME, GOD SENT FORTH HIS SON, MADE OF A WOMAN, MADE UNDER THE LAW, TO REDEEM THEM THAT WERE UNDER THE LAW, THAT WE MIGHT RECEIVE THE ADOPTION OF SONS.

Galatians 4:4-5

Scriptures About Salvation

Romans 10:9-10

That if thou shalt confess with thy mouth the Lord Jesus, and shalt believe in thine heart that God hath raised him from the dead, thou shalt be saved. For with the heart man believeth unto righteousness; and with the mouth confession is made unto salvation.

1 John 4:9

In this was manifested the love of God toward us, because that God sent his only begotten Son into the world, that we might live through him.

Mark 16:16

He that believeth and is baptized shall be saved; but he that believeth not shall be damned.

Acts 4:12

Neither is there salvation in any other: for there is none other name under heaven given among men, whereby we must be saved.

John 3:16

For God so loved the world, that he gave his only begotten Son, that whosoever believeth in him should not perish, but have everlasting life.

John 6:37

All that the Father giveth me shall come to me; and him that cometh to me I will in no wise cast out.

John 6:47

Verily, verily, I say unto you, He that believeth on me hath everlasting life.

Acts 2:38

Then Peter said unto them, Repent, and be baptized every one of you in the name of Jesus Christ for the remission of sins, and ye shall receive the gift of the Holy Ghost.

2 Timothy 1:9

Who hath saved us, and called [us] with an holy calling, not according to our works, but according to his own purpose and grace, which was given us in Christ Jesus before the world began.

Romans 1:16

For I am not ashamed of the gospel of Christ: for it is the power of God unto salvation to every one that believeth; to the Jew first, and also to the Greek.

John 5:24

Verily, verily, I say unto you, He that heareth my word, and believeth on him that sent me, hath everlasting life, and shall not come into condemnation; but is passed from death unto life.

2 Timothy 1:10

But is now made manifest by the appearing of our Savior Jesus Christ, who hath abolished death, and hath brought life and immortality to light through the gospel.

Acts 15:11

But we believe that through the grace of the Lord Jesus Christ we shall be saved, even as they.

Hebrews 2:10
For it became him, for whom [are] all things, and by whom [are] all things, in bringing many sons unto glory, to make the captain of their salvation perfect through sufferings.

Hebrews 5:9
And being made perfect, he became the author of eternal salvation unto all them that obey him.

Ephesians 2:8
For by grace are ye saved through faith; and that not of yourselves: [it is] the gift of God:

Acts 13:47
For so hath the Lord commanded us, [saying], I have set thee to be a light of the Gentiles, that thou shouldest be for salvation unto the ends of the earth.

Ephesians 2:8
For by grace are ye saved through faith; and that not of yourselves: [it is] the gift of God:

1 Corinthians 6:11
And such were some of you: but ye are washed, but ye are sanctified, but ye are justified in the name of the Lord Jesus, and by the Spirit of our God.

CHRISTOLOGY

"the branch of Christian theology relating to the person, nature, and role of Christ" (Oxford Languages).

Understanding Christology

John 3:16: For God so loved the world, that he gave his only Son, that whoever believes in him should not perish but have eternal life.

Christ + connective -o- + -logy.

Christology
A particular theory or viewpoint within the field of Christology, e.g. Chalcedonian Christology, Arian Christology, etc.. (uncountable) A field of study within Christian theology which is concerned with the nature of Jesus Christ, particularly with how the divine and human are related in his person.
Source: etymologeek.com

Christology
Christology, Christian reflection, teaching, and doctrine concerning Jesus of Nazareth. Christology is the part of theology that is concerned with the nature and work of Jesus, including such matters as the Incarnation, the Resurrection, and his human and divine natures and their relationship. The underlying methodological assumption of Christology is that the New Testament contains the authentic and accurate record of Jesus, both explicitly and implicitly.
Source: Encyclopedia Britannica

Christology is the branch of theology that deals with the study of Christ. There are three branches of Christology.

Ontological	Functional	Soteriological
The study of the nature of Christ Jesus.	The study of Jesus' works, including miracles He performed.	The study of salvation as it relates to Christianity or Christ's finished works.

Trinitarianism vs. Unitarianism

The Great Christological question is: What is the relationship between YAHWEH and Jesus? Many religious denominations have been split because of this question, just as many denominations have been established on some man's answers to this question. The most asked question is—are Jesus and God one and the same? There are two doctrines centered around this question. They are:

Trinitarianism	Unitarianism
Theology of God being one God in three co-distinctions: the Father, Son (Jesus Christ) and the Holy Spirit.	Theological movement that asserts that God is one entity, not three-in-one.

Most believers ascribe to Trinitarianism, but the million dollar question is, how can God and Jesus be one person?
1. God is Spirit.
2. Jesus is the living Word of God.
3. Holy Spirit is the Spirit of God.

Think of it this way. As humans, we are tri-part beings, consisting of a body, a spirit and a soul. These are all three expressions of one person; right? While your body can be distinguished from your soul, they both work in tandem with one another. Nevertheless, if your soul leaves your body, your body would cease to exist. The same is true for your soul and your spirit. Your spirit is the eternal side of you; you are a breath of God. This is why you are eternal! But without your spirit, your soul (mind, will and emotions) could not exist. A unitarian concept of humans being one entity would suggest that you (your spirit) and your body, along with your soul, of course, are all one. Howbeit, this would also suggest that upon death (of the body), the individual would cease to exist or the individual would have to entirely (body, soul and spirit) be translated to his or her forever home.

Other facts to consider:
1. The Old Testament refers to the preexistence of Christ (see Exodus 17:6, Numbers 20:8-11, Numbers 21:5-6).
2. The New Testament refers to the preexistence of Christ before He ever inhabited a body (see John 17:5, 1 Corinthians 15:47, Ephesians 4:9-10, Galatians 4:4).
3. The New Testament preaches a trinitarian concept (see Matthew 12:28, Matthew 28:19-20, John 20:22, Romans 1:4, Romans 8:9).
4. The scriptures use many types and shadows to represent Jesus (Exodus 17:6, Numbers 20:8-11, 1 Corinthians 6:9, Jude 5).
5. Jesus is referred to as God many times in the New Testament (see John 1:1, John 10:28, Titus 2:13, Hebrews 1:8, 2 Peter 1:1).

THE SPIRIT WORLD

Riddled with mystery, the spirit world has always been a source of debate for both believers and unbelievers alike. The discussion of spirits has divided the church, with some theologians firmly asserting that Christians cannot have demons, while other faiths assert that Christians can have demons. But what is the spirit world like?

First and foremost, let's establish this; the realm of the spirit is more real than the world as we know it. We have to remember that we are tri-part beings.
1. We are spirits.
2. We have a soul.
3. We possess a body.

Body	Soul	Spirit
Death	Tongue	Life

And because we are spirits, we are naturally spiritual. Additionally, when we leave our bodies (first death), our spirits lose consciousness of the natural world, and immediately gain consciousness of the spirit realm (see 2 Corinthians 5:8). All the same, the Bible tells us that life and death are in the power of the tongue. It is our confession, coupled with the yielding of our hearts that will determine what we inherit. Keep in mind that an inheritance comes from a father. The children of God receive a kingly inheritance from God because He is their Father, but the children of Satan will also receive an inheritance from him; their inheritance is called death.

Spiritual Mediators

The spirit realm often uses mankind as a medium between two worlds, but hear me—God cast Satan and his angels out of Heaven, therefore, Heaven does not use mankind to mediate between Heaven and Hell, even though Satan tries to use humans as mediators between his kingdom and God's Kingdom (see chart below).

Kingdom of Darkness	Kingdom of Man	Kingdom of God
Satan/Unclean Spirits	Mankind	YAHWEH/Angels
Spirit Realm	**Natural Realm**	**Spirit Realm**

Because neither Satan nor his angels have earth-suits, they cannot naturally reach mankind, therefore, they have to reach us through a medium (spiritualist). The medium is a person who has become conscious of the spirit realm and yields himself or herself (consciously and physically) to unclean spirits; this way, they can express themselves in the Earth.

Kingdom of Darkness	Medium/Mediator	Kingdom of Man
Satan/Unclean Spirits	Witch/Sorcerer/Warlock/Rebel	Mankind

The Prophet of God, the Intercessor and the prophetic person (yielded believer) stand in as mediums or mediators between God and mankind.

Kingdom of Man	Medium/Mediator	Kingdom of God
Satan/Unclean Spirits	Prophet/Believer/Intercessor	Mankind

What this tells us is that information is always traveling between each kingdom, but in order for each kingdom to communicate, there has to be a mediator who yields himself or herself to that particular kingdom.

Angelogy vs. Demonology

Angelogy	Demonology
The term "angelogy" comes from two Greek terms, namely, aggelos (pronounced angelos) meaning "messenger" or "angel" and logos meaning "word," "matter," or "thing." In Christian systematic theology it is used to refer to the study of the biblical doctrine of angels. It includes such topics as the origin, existence, and nature of angels, classifications of angels, the service and works of angels as well the existence, activity, and judgment of Satan and demons (as fallen or wicked angels). Some theologians, however, treat Satan and demons under a separate heading, namely, demonology.	A demon is an evil spirit, or devil, in the ordinary English usage of the term. This definition is, however, only approximate. In polytheistic religions the line between gods and demons is a shifting one: there are both good demons and gods who do evil. In monotheistic systems, evil spirits may be accepted as servants of the one God, so that demonology is bound up with angelogy and theology proper, or they may be elevated to the rank of opponents of God, in which case their status as diabolic powers differs from that of the demons in polytheism. Moreover, in none of the languages of the ancient Near

The Spirit World

Angelogy	Demonology
An angel is a spirit being created by God and commissioned by Him for some special purpose in accordance with the outworking of His plan (e.g., Col 1:16; Heb 1:14). They have enormous, though limited (as a creature) power and knowledge. They are referred to as "messengers" in both the Old and New Testaments and as such they carry out the work of God. Though some scholars have denied their personhood, it is clear from Scripture that they do indeed have personality; they think (1 Peter 1:12), feel (Luke 2:13), and choose (Jude 6), and holy angels render intelligent and excellent praise to God. They are of a higher order than man, as Psalm 8:4-5 explains, but they are inferior to Christ (2 Sam 14:20; Luke 20:36; Heb 1). Apparently they are unable to procreate (Matt 22:30). In the Old Testament angels are also referred to as the "heavenly host," "sons of God," and "holy ones" (1 Samuel 17:45; Job 1:6; 2:1; Psalm 89:5, 7). The first expression, "heavenly host" relates to their innumerable number and power to defend God's people (cf. Heb 12:22). The second expression, "sons of God" highlights their close relationship to God, their godlike qualities, and the capacity in which they function before him. The third expression, "holy ones," underscores their pure moral character.	East, including Hebrew, is there any one general term equivalent to English "demon." In general, the notion of a demon in the ancient Near East was of a being less powerful than a god and less endowed with individuality. Whereas the great gods are accorded regular public worship, demons are not; they are dealt with in magic rites in individual cases of human suffering, which is their particular sphere. The Israelite conception of demons, as it existed in the popular mind or the literary imagination, resembled in some ways that held elsewhere. Demons live in deserts or ruins (Lev. 16:10; Isa. 13:21; 34:14). They inflict sickness on men (Ps. 91:5–6). They trouble men's minds (Saul; 1 Sam. 16:15, 23) and deceive them (1 Kings 22:22–23) – but nevertheless these evil spirits are sent by the Lord. The mysterious being who attacks Jacob in Genesis 32:25ff. exhibits a trait which a very widespread belief associated with certain demons, who are spirits of the night and must perish at dawn. Even in Israelite popular religion, however, there seems to have been relatively little fear of the spirits of the dead. The Bible often mentions the shades of the dead, but "the congregation of the shades" (Prov. 21:16) carries on a shadowy existence below, and does not seem to trouble the living. Some features of the Israelite cult bear a formal resemblance to apotropaic measures employed in other religions. Thus, the bells on the robe of the high priest (Ex. 28:33–35) recall the use of

Angelogy	Demonology
	bells in other cultures in the belief that their tinkling keeps off demons. So, also, horns (Ex. 19:16; Lev. 25:9; et al.), incense (Lev. 16:12–13), smearing of doorposts (Ex. 12:7), the color blue (Num. 15:38), written scripture-texts (phylacteries; Deut. 6:8; 11:18) – all have parallels elsewhere as devices to ward off evil spirits. In a given case, however, it is often extremely difficult to say to what extent any of these devices were consciously used for protection against demons at a particular period.
Source: Bible.org	Source: Jewish Virtual Library

Angel

"one of a class of spiritual beings, attendants and messengers of God," a c. 1300 fusion of Old English engel (with hard -g-) and Old French angele. Both are from Late Latin angelus, from Greek angelos, literally "messenger, envoy, one that announces," in the New Testament "divine messenger," which is possibly related to angaros "mounted courier," both from an unknown Oriental word (Watkins compares Sanskrit ajira- "swift;" Klein suggests Semitic sources). Used in Scriptural translations for Hebrew mal'akh (yehowah) "messenger (of Jehovah)," from base l-'-k "to send." An Old English word for it was aerendgast, literally "errand-spirit."

Of persons, "one who is loving, gracious, or lovely," by 1590s. The medieval English gold coin (a new issue of the noble, first struck 1465 by Edward VI) was so called for the image of archangel Michael slaying the dragon, which was stamped on it. It was the coin given to patients who had been "touched" for the King's Evil. Angel food cake is from 1881; angel dust "phencyclidine" is from 1968.

Source: Online Etymology Dictionary

Demon

c. 1200, "an evil spirit, malignant supernatural being, an incubus, a devil," from Latin daemon "spirit," from Greek daimōn "deity, divine power; lesser god; guiding spirit, tutelary deity" (sometimes including souls of the dead); "one's genius, lot, or fortune;" from PIE *dai-mon- "divider, provider" (of fortunes or destinies), from root *da- "to divide."

The malignant sense is because the Greek word was used (with daimonion) in Christian Greek translations and the Vulgate for "god of the heathen, heathen idol" and also for "unclean spirit." Jewish authors earlier had employed the Greek word in this sense, using it to render shedim "lords, idols" in the Septuagint, and Matthew viii.31 has daimones, translated as deofol in Old English, feend or deuil in Middle English. Another Old English word for this was hellcniht, literally "hell-knight."

The usual ancient Greek sense, "supernatural agent or intelligence lower than a god, ministering spirit" is attested in English from 1560s and is sometimes written daemon or daimon for purposes of distinction. Meaning "destructive or hideous person" is from 1610s; as "an evil agency personified" (rum, etc.) from 1712.

Source: Online Etymology Dictionary

Greek Word Study	
Angel (aggelos)	**Demon (daimonion)**
from an unused root meaning to despatch as a deputy; a messenger; specifically, of God, i.e. an angel (also a prophet, priest or teacher):--ambassador, angel, king, messenger.	probably demon
Source: Strong's Concordance	Source: Strong's Concordance

Hebrew Word Study	
Angel (mal'akh/mal'ak)	**Demon (shed)**
a messenger, generally a (supernatural) messenger from God, an angel, conveying news or behests from God to men.	an evil-spirit, demon; a heathen deity.
Source: Strong's Concordance	Source: Strong's Concordance

VISUAL CHARTS

Messiah	Message		Messenger
YAHWEH	Message	**Angel (Messenger)**	Mankind
Satan	Message	**Devil (Messenger)**	Mankind
Satan	Message	**Mankind**	**YAHWEH**

The Creation of Angels

Which came first—the chicken or the egg? We've all run across this question, and if we are to be honest, most of us haven't tried to answer it because it just seems pointless. Nevertheless, these types of questions do create somewhat of a stir, and it is for this reason that I pose this question—when did angels come into existence? After all, the Bible does not expressly detail the creation of angels, even though the book of Genesis does talk about the creation of man. But the book of Genesis does answer this question indirectly when the author details the order in which God created everything. First, God created the Heavens and the Earth. This is because before God creates a living creature, He first prepares a place for it. How did God create angels? He created them in the Beginning. Who is God? He is Alpha and Omega, the Beginning and the End. Consider the process that we undertake, as humans, to create something. First, it starts off as a problem. For example, maybe you were driving your car one day and realized that your air conditioner was no longer working. You didn't necessarily have the time or the cash to put your car in the repair shop, so you started being creative. What could you do to bring yourself immediate relief? At first, you let your car's windows down, but the flow of air that came into your car was everything but cool. All the same, as you got closer to your destination, you found yourself riding more through neighborhoods and zones where you had to travel no more than 25-45 miles per hour, and you had to keep stopping at stop signs. By the time you reached your destination, you were drenched in sweat. And one day while dealing with the harsh summer sun, you had an idea. You stopped by your local supermarket and bought a large bag of ice. You then took that ice home and placed it in your freezer, but before you went to bed that night, you grabbed your cooler from the garage, filled it with the ice you'd purchased and placed it in your car with the windows up. In the morning, you grabbed your portable fan and took it with you to your vehicle before leaving out for work. You turned the fan on, and the precipitation from the night before seemed to work together with the fan to create an air-conditioned like feel. That's when an idea began to emerge. Maybe, you could create a portable air conditioner that ran completely off ice cubes! You hired an artist to draw up a sketch of your idea, you saved your money, and before long, you were able to hire a patent attorney. Seven years later, you found yourself signing one of many deals with a manufacturer and you cashed your first million-dollar check. In other words, your solution started off as a problem.

Looking back at the creation of angels, God first determined that there was a problem He needed them to solve. In other words, they are purposeful creatures, just as we are. But before creating angels, He first needed to create a domain for them, so in the Beginning, God created the Heavens and the Earth. He created the Heavens first, meaning, He created angels before He created man.

But wait. God is Spirit, and the word "spirit" means "breath" or "wind." Since He created us (man) a little lower than angels, and He created us in His image, I think it's safe to say that they were also created in His image. And since we are spirits locked inside of bodies, we can safely summarize that angels are spirits; they are the individual breaths of God. And each angel has a purpose (assignment or reason for which he was created).

Types of Angels

Seraphim	Cherubim	Thrones
Dominions	Virtues	Powers and Authorities
Principalities (Rulers)	Archangels	Angels

ANGELS WERE CREATED TO MANAGE THE HEAVENS.

Crime	Judgment
Genesis 6:1-2	**Jude 1:6**
And it came to pass, when men began to multiply on the face of the earth, and daughters were born unto them, that the sons of God saw the daughters of men that they *were* fair; and they took them wives of all which they chose.	And the angels which kept not their first estate, but left their own habitation, he hath reserved in everlasting chains under darkness unto the judgment of the great day.

Please note that Jude 1:6 wasn't just referring to the angels who left their post to marry women, but the angels who were in Heaven who abandoned their assignments to follow Satan.

Facts About Angels

1. Angels rejoice every time a sinner gets saved (see Luke 15:10).
2. Angels were created by God (see Colossians 6:16).
3. Sometimes, angels disguise themselves in flesh and visit people (Hebrews 13:2).
4. Angels have the freedom of will (see Jude 1:6).
5. Angels existed before humans (see Job 38:4-7).
6. Angels are not all-knowing (omniscient) (see 1 Peter 1:12).
7. We do have guardian angels (see Psalm 91:11-12).
8. The Bible only mentioned two angels by name; they are Michael and Gabriel.
9. Angels have ranks (see Daniel 10:13).
10. Angels serve as ministering spirits (see Hebrews 1:14).
11. There are thousands upon thousands of angels (see Psalm 68:17).
12. Angels do not have genders because they are not made of matter, but they are referenced using masculine verbiage (see Genesis 18:2).
13. Angels are immortal (see Luke 20:34-36).
14. All angels don't look the same (see Isaiah 6:2).
15. Lucifer was an archangel like Michael, and since angels come in rank, Michael was the angel who ranked high enough to confront and bind Satan.

The Great Angelic Fall

Lucifer was a beautifully designed angel. He was so beautiful that even he became smitten with his own reflection (see Ezekiel 28:17). He was a covering angel (see Ezekiel 28:14), and not just any angel, he was "the anointed cherub." In other words, YAHWEH had entrusted Lucifer with a great responsibility, and to know what this responsibility was, all we have to do is look to the scriptures. Ezekiel 28:1-14 tells us that Lucifer's body was made of precious jewels and tabrets. Now, understand this—everything God created has purpose attached to it. Nothing is created to just exist; everything is created as a part of a system, and everything God created has a function. Therefore, the jewels on Lucifer's body had a purpose; the same is true for the tabrets (musical instruments). For example, every jewel ever created by God has a unique way in which it responds to light. According to 1 John 1:5, God is Light. John 1:4 tells us that this light was the life of man. So, in the Most High God, there was life. What this means is that before the creation of man, Lucifer had insight into God's plans. Whenever Lucifer would go into God's presence, His body would automatically absorb revelation; his body would soak up the glory of God. His assignment was to then take what he'd absorbed and serve as a messenger to God's angels; these were the angels that he had been anointed to cover. When the angels would see the glory of God radiating through Lucifer, they would bow and began to worship God. But Lucifer, looking out at the congregation began to covet this worship for himself.

And let's not forget his tabrets (pipes, instruments). When the angels would bow in worship, Lucifer's body would serve as an instrument, allowing their praises to pass through him. This would usher in the presence of God. All the same, God would speak to His angels through Lucifer, meaning He would sing back to them. He would communicate with them through Lucifer. But again, Lucifer began to covet this worship for himself. He looked at his reflection and realized just how beautiful he was! He was a uniquely designed angel, and he started to believe that he himself could be and should be a god.

Fun fact: Lucifer was likely one of the angels depicted on the ark of the covenant. Again, he was the anointed cherub who covered. You'll notice that the angels on the mercy seat are peering down into the ark; this represents them looking into the secrets or the mysteries of God. Lucifer then took what he saw and began to traffic it to God's angels (see Ezekiel 28:5). In short, he exchanged the glory or revelations of God for the angels' alliances. He told them that they could be like God; he sold them the idea that they didn't need God to flourish, and one-third of God's angels bought into this lie. Hear me—he would steal these angels away into the darkness; this was outside the presence of Light (God). This was a territory not yet addressed by God. This is why he is prince over the kingdom of darkness.

The Kingdom of Darkness

Kingdom of Darkness	Kingdom of Man	Kingdom of God
Fallen Angels	Humans	Good Angels
Bad Breaths	←—→	Good Breaths

Again, Satan lied to the angels he had been anointed to cover. Remember, he'd decided that he wanted to be like God; he wanted to be worshiped, and he wanted to be independent of God's influence. Howbeit, he had an assignment.. He was an archangel; in other words, he was a high-ranking angel. Remember when God created the Heavens and the Earth, and darkness was upon the face of the deep? Where did the darkness come from? First and foremost, darkness is not a substance; it is not the existence of dark matter. It has no real existence. It simply means to be void of light. Again, who is God? He is Light (and not in the way that pagan religions refer to Him). Who was Lucifer? He was God's Light-Bearer. He was like an armor bearer for God, only he carried the glory of God through the many gems that covered his body. And hear me—darkness in and of itself isn't necessarily an evil place; it's what takes place in the darkness (outside of God's presence and influence) that makes it wicked. What Lucifer used to do was steal God's angels away into the darkness, and it was there that he sold them some truths and facts in his attempt to create his own followers. Why did he do this? Because he wanted to be like God. He was consumed with envy!

Again, darkness was just a space that hadn't yet been touched by God! When Lucifer fell and became Satan, he lost his job as Light-Bearer, therefore he became increasingly dark and so did the angels that served him. This is why they love darkness! Also, what grows in the kingdom of darkness cannot grow in the Kingdom of God. Think of the things that grow in the dark in the Earth. Mold mostly grows in the dark because the UV lights from the sun would kill it; the same is true for mildew. Mildew can be eliminated by fresh air and direct exposure to sunlight. Howbeit, most plants need sunlight to survive and to thrive. This is a picture of two kingdoms; what flourishes in the light dies in the darkness, but what flourishes in the darkness is destroyed by light.

And of course, the works of the flesh thrive in the darkness, but the fruits of the Spirit thrive in the Kingdom of God!

The Kingdom of God

Colossians 1:13-14

Who hath delivered us from the power of darkness, and hath translated us into the kingdom of his dear Son: in whom we have redemption through his blood, eve the forgiveness of sins.

1 Peter 2:9

But you are a chosen race, a royal priesthood, a holy nation, a people for God's own possession, so that you may proclaim the excellencies of Him who has called you out of darkness into His marvelous light.

Synonyms of Light		
Glory	Illuminated	Luminous
Glowing	Clear	Sun

| Radiant | Revelation | Day |

In the book of 1 John 1:5, we find the author referring to God as Light. John 1:4 says that "In Him was life, and that life was the light of men." What does this mean? In truth, when we hear the Bible referring to God as Light, we use our humanistic reasoning to try and imagine what God must "look" like. Nevertheless, God is Spirit; He's not just "a" Spirit, He is Spirit. What this means is that our natural eyes cannot comprehend Him, for He is spiritually discerned. And of course, we see a lot of occultic and pagan movements referring to their "god" as light. Consequently, we (as the Church) try to avoid certain words and phraseology out of fear of offending others in the faith. Howbeit, the Bible refers to God as Light, just not in the sense that we comprehend the word "light." In other words, God is not just a bright sparkle that we can see; He is the Source of everything and the Revealer of all things. Interestingly enough, some of the characteristics of natural light are very similar to His characteristics.

Natural Light	**God (Light)**
Travels at 186,282 miles per second. Nothing can travel faster than light.	Is Omnipresent.
Light travels in a straight line.	If we trust in the Lord with all of our heart, do not lean to our own understanding, and we acknowledge Him in all of our ways, He will make our paths straight. In short, He will let us walk with Him.
Reveals what's hiding in the darkness.	Reveals what's hiding in the darkness.
Has no mass, but it does have momentum.	Has no mass, but it does have momentum.
Light must enter our eyes in order for us to see.	God must enter into our hearts in order for us to see clearly.

So, what exactly is the Kingdom of God? In short, the Kingdom of God is the will of God. Think of it this way—you have a mind, and within that mind, you have a belief system, a set of plans, a ton of memories, a measure of confidence, a few fears here and there and the list goes on. This is your garden. And what you pick from that garden or, better yet, believe ultimately manifests itself as your reality. In other words, it breaks the ground between the unseen and manifests itself in the visible realm, where it begins to produce more and more fruit in your life. This fruit is called your reality. Your reality is your kingdom. It manifests itself through the expression of your will, the confession of your lips and through the people who you surround yourself with. We often say, "Your Kingdom come, your will be done" when referencing God in prayer. In short, like us, God has a mind. If and when He thinks something up, He pulls it out of Himself through the expression of His will. In short, He speaks a thing and it is so! This means that whatever God desires, He pulls it out of Himself. He is good, so everything He pulls out of Himself is good! Unfortunately for us, our hearts are deceptively wicked, therefore, whenever we pull a thought out of our hearts and we cause that thought to materialize itself into something tangible, it has oftentimes been contaminated by our perversion. Again, the Kingdom of God is the will of God expressed.

Unlike the kingdom of man, the Kingdom of God cannot be "seen." Luke 17:20-23 reads, "And when he was demanded of the Pharisees, hen the kingdom of God should come, he answered them and said, The kingdom of God cometh not with observation: Neither shall they say, Lo here! Or lo there! For, behold, the kingdom of God is within you."

Other facts about the Kingdom include:
1. The Kingdom of God has to be received (Mark 10:13-16).
2. Jesus established the Kingdom of God on Earth when He came into the world.
3. Our God is King of kings and Lord of lords, meaning, every kingdom has to submit to Him, including the kingdom of darkness.
4. The word "Kingdom" has nothing to do with a specific locale, it simply denotes the subjects over which God reigns; it is the will of God, and wherever you find God's will, you will find God's presence!
5. The Greek word for "kingdom" is "basileia" and it literally means "the realm in which a king sovereignly rules" (Source: HELPS Word-studies).

Types of Demons

The angels who stole away into the darkness with Lucifer all had assignments that had been given to them by God. All the same, there were different types of angels with varying functions. Therefore, when they fell, they all became specific types of demons.

This list of demons are oftentimes found (and cast out) in standard deliverance sessions.

Rejection	Abandonment	Rebellion
Fear of Rejection	Fear of Abandonment	Pride
Witchcraft	Fear (Kingdom)	Anger/Rage
Guilt	Shame	Condemnation

Vagabond	Orphan	Python
Leviathan	Self Rejection	Self Hatred
Hurt/ Deep Hurt	Broken Heart	Wounded Spirit
Sadness	Rape	Molestation
Incest	Mermaid	Spirit Spouse
Lust and Whoredom	Loneliness	Homosexuality
Fornication	Depression/Heaviness	Murder
Suicide	Death/Premature Death	Envy/Jealousy
Discouragement	Frustration	Trauma
Confusion	Suspicion	Gossip/Slander
Jezebel	Ahab	Athaliah
Infirmity	Control	Antichrist
Religious Spirits	Bitterness/Root of Bitterness	Memory Recall
Mind-Binding	Mind-Blinding	Mind Control
Incubus	Succubus	Restlessness/Insomnia

Believe it or not, this is just a short list, and yes, many of them are called or referred to by their functions. For example, the spirit of confusion brings confusion, but it typically works with other spirits to cause calamity.

Facts About Demons

1. The "sons of God" mentioned in Genesis 6:2 were fallen angels (demons).
2. Like Satan, demons are neither omniscient (all-knowing), omnipresent (ubiquitous)
3. or omnipotent (all-powerful).
4. Christians can be demonized; the difference is unbelievers can be possessed by demons, while believers can be only be oppressed by demons.
5. Sacrifices to idols, according to the Bible, were actually sacrifices to demons (Leviticus 17:7, Deuteronomy 32:17).
6. The Bible references evil spirits that were "from the Lord." These include the evil spirit that tormented King Saul (see 1 Samuel 16:14) and an evil spirit that went forth to bring about the destruction of Ahab by being a lying spirit in the mouths of Jezebel's prophets

(see 1 Kings 22:22). What this tells us is that while the kingdom of darkness is antithetical to the Kingdom of God, unclean spirits can and do submit themselves to God.
7. Some demons are permanently confined (see Jude 1:6); some demons, along with Satan, will be temporarily confined for a thousand years (see Revelation 20).
8. Even though Satan employed Antichrist spirits, both Satan and his demons believe in Jesus (see James 2:19).
9. The final destination for demons is the lake of fire (see Revelation 20:10).
10. Evil angels (aka demons) do impersonate good angels (2 Corinthians 11:14).

Demon Stories in the Bible

Matthew 8:28-34

And when he was come to the other side into the country of the Gergesenes, there met him two possessed with devils, coming out of the tombs, exceeding fierce, so that no man might pass by that way. And, behold, they cried out, saying, What have we to do with thee, Jesus, thou Son of God? Art thou come hither to torment us before the time? And there was a good way off from them an herd of many swine feeding. So the devils besought him, saying, If thou cast us out, suffer us to go away into the herd of swine. And he said unto them, Go. And when they were come out, they went into the herd of swine: and, behold, the whole herd of swine ran violently down a steep place into the sea, and perished in the waters. And they that kept them fled, and went their ways into the city, and told every thing, and what was befallen to the possessed of the devils. And, behold, the whole city came out to meet Jesus: and when they saw him, they besought him that he would depart out of their coasts.

Luke 8:26-33

And they arrived at the country of the Gadarenes, which is over against Galilee. And when he went forth to land, there met him out of the city a certain man, which had devils long time, and ware no clothes, neither abode in any house, but in the tombs. When he saw Jesus, he cried out, and fell down before him, and with a loud voice said, What have I to do with thee, Jesus, thou Son of God most high? I beseech thee, torment me not. (For he had commanded the unclean spirit to come out of the man. For oftentimes it had caught him: and he was kept bound with chains and in fetters; and he brake the bands, and was driven of the devil into the wilderness.) And Jesus asked him, saying, What is thy name? And he said, Legion: because many devils were entered into him. And they besought him that he would not command them to go out into the deep.

> And there was there an herd of many swine feeding on the mountain: and they besought him that he would suffer them to enter into them. And he suffered them. Then went the devils out of the man, and entered into the swine: and the herd ran violently down a steep place into the lake, and were choked.

Note: The aforementioned scriptures are two separate accounts of the same story; they are Matthew's account of the incident and Luke's account of the incident. You've probably noticed that in Matthew's recounting of the incident, he speaks of two-demon possessed men that were in the tombs on that day, whereas, Luke speaks of only one demoniac. Which story is accurate? They both are! In Matthew's account, he seems to be more focused on or fascinated by the unclean spirits that spoke through both men, however, Luke seems to be more focused on one of the men. In his account, he never said that there was only one man at the tombs that day; instead, his story centers around a "certain man." Luke takes notice of the fact that this particular man was naked. So, we can gather that both men saw the same thing, but they were intrigued by different aspects of the same event. What's the point here? It's simple—if you come across what appears to be a contradiction when studying the Bible, examine the text closer. Don't be so quick to point out what appears to be a discrepancy. Instead, closely examine the text and pay attention to the:

1. Author's style of writing
2. The entirety of the story. Don't select a paragraph of text; be sure to read the story in its entirety to get the context.
3. The Bible translation that you're using.

1 Kings 22:19-23

> But the Spirit of the LORD departed from Saul, and an evil spirit from the LORD troubled him. And he said, Hear thou therefore the word of the LORD: I saw the LORD sitting on his throne, and all the host of heaven standing by him on his right hand and on his left. And the LORD said, Who shall persuade Ahab, that he may go up and fall at Ramothgilead? And one said on this manner, and another said on that manner. And there came forth a spirit, and stood before the LORD, and said, I will persuade him. And the LORD said unto him, Wherewith? And he said, I will go forth, and I will be a lying spirit in the mouth of all his prophets. And he said, Thou shalt persuade him, and prevail also: go forth, and do so. Now therefore, behold, the LORD hath put a lying spirit in the mouth of all these thy prophets, and the LORD hath spoken evil concerning thee.

1 Samuel 16:14-23

But the Spirit of the LORD departed from Saul, and an evil spirit from the LORD troubled him. And Saul's servants said unto him, Behold now, an evil spirit from God troubleth thee. Let our lord now command thy servants, which are before thee, to seek out a man, who is a cunning player on an harp: and it shall come to pass, when the evil spirit from God is upon thee, that he shall play with his hand, and thou shalt be well. And Saul said unto his servants, Provide me now a man that can play well, and bring him to me. Then answered one of the servants, and said, Behold, I have seen a son of Jesse the Bethlehemite, that is cunning in playing, and a mighty valiant man, and a man of war, and prudent in matters, and a comely person, and the LORD is with him. Wherefore Saul sent messengers unto Jesse, and said, Send me David thy son, which is with the sheep. And Jesse took an ass laden with bread, and a bottle of wine, and a kid, and sent them by David his son unto Saul. And David came to Saul, and stood before him: and he loved him greatly; and he became his armourbearer. And Saul sent to Jesse, saying, Let David, I pray thee, stand before me; for he hath found favour in my sight. And it came to pass, when the evil spirit from God was upon Saul, that David took an harp, and played with his hand: so Saul was refreshed, and was well, and the evil spirit departed from him.

1 Samuel 19:8-10

And there was war again: and David went out, and fought with the Philistines, and slew them with a great slaughter; and they fled from him. And the evil spirit from the LORD was upon Saul, as he sat in his house with his javelin in his hand: and David played with *his* hand. And Saul sought to smite David even to the wall with the javelin; but he slipped away out of Saul's presence, and he smote the javelin into the wall: and David fled, and escaped that night.

Judges 9:22-25

When Abimelech had reigned three years over Israel, Then God sent an evil spirit between Abimelech and the men of Shechem; and the men of Shechem dealt treacherously with Abimelech: That the cruelty *done* to the threescore and ten sons of Jerubbaal might come, and their blood be laid upon Abimelech their brother, which slew them; and upon the men of Shechem, which aided him in the killing of his brethren. And the men of Shechem set liers in wait for him in the top of the mountains, and they robbed all that came along that way by them: and it was told Abimelech.

Acts 19:30-20

Then certain of the vagabond Jews, exorcists, took upon them to call over them which had evil spirits the name of the Lord Jesus, saying, We adjure you by Jesus whom Paul preacheth. And there were seven sons of one Sceva, a Jew, and chief of the priests, which did so. And the evil spirit answered and said, Jesus I know, and Paul I know; but who are ye? And the man in whom the evil spirit was leaped on them, and overcame them, and prevailed against them, so that they fled out of that house naked and wounded. And this was known to all the Jews and Greeks also dwelling at Ephesus; and fear fell on them all, and the name of the Lord Jesus was magnified. And many that believed came, and confessed, and shewed their deeds. Many of them also which used curious arts brought their books together, and burned them before all men: and they counted the price of them, and found it fifty thousand pieces of silver. So mightily grew the word of God and prevailed.

Mark 9:14-29

And when he came to his disciples, he saw a great multitude about them, and the scribes questioning with them. And straightway all the people, when they beheld him, were greatly amazed, and running to him saluted him. And he asked the scribes, What question ye with them? And one of the multitude answered and said, Master, I have brought unto thee my son, which hath a dumb spirit; And wheresoever he taketh him, he teareth him: and he foameth, and gnasheth with his teeth, and pineth away: and I spake to thy disciples that they should cast him out; and they could not. He answereth him, and saith, O faithless generation, how long shall I be with you? how long shall I suffer you? bring him unto me. And they brought him unto him: and when he saw him, straightway the spirit tare him; and he fell on the ground, and wallowed foaming. And he asked his father, How long is it ago since this came unto him? And he said, Of a child. And ofttimes it hath cast him into the fire, and into the waters, to destroy him: but if thou canst do any thing, have compassion on us, and help us. Jesus said unto him, If thou canst believe, all things are possible to him that believeth. And straightway the father of the child cried out, and said with tears, Lord, I believe; help thou mine unbelief. When Jesus saw that the people came running together, he rebuked the foul spirit, saying unto him, Thou dumb and deaf spirit, I charge thee, come out of him, and enter no more into him. And the spirit cried, and rent him sore, and came out of him: and he was as one dead; insomuch that many said, He is dead. But Jesus took him by the hand, and lifted him up; and he arose. And when he was come into the house, his disciples asked him privately, Why could not we cast him out? And he said unto them, This kind can come forth by nothing, but by prayer and fasting.

The Spirit World

Acts 16:16-18

And it came to pass, as we went to prayer, a certain damsel possessed with a spirit of divination met us, which brought her masters much gain by soothsaying: The same followed Paul and us, and cried, saying, These men are the servants of the most high God, which shew unto us the way of salvation. And this did she many days. But Paul, being grieved, turned and said to the spirit, I command thee in the name of Jesus Christ to come out of her. And he came out the same hour.

Popup Memory Test

In the space provided below, list as many demonic types as you can remember.

FALSE DOCTRINE AND BIBLICAL MISINTERPRETATION

"In the beginning was the Word, and the Word was with God, and the Word was God."
(John 1:1)

The Greek word for "doctrine" is "didaché" and it means:
- teaching
- what is taught

The foundation of Christian doctrine asserts that:
- One God (YAHWEH) who exists in three expressions: the Father, the Son and the Holy Spirit.
- The virgin birth of Christ.
- The death and bodily resurrection of Jesus Christ.
- The atonement for our sins as a result of Christ's crucifixion.
- The second coming of Christ Jesus.
- The Bible is inerrant (without error).

Nevertheless, there is what the Bible refers to as "false doctrine." False doctrine is as it sounds—false! Consider this—Jesus is:
1. The Living Word of God.
2. The Truth.

Therefore, any doctrine that promotes:
1. That Jesus Christ isn't the Son of God is false!
2. That Jesus Christ isn't God is false!
3. Any other Messiah other than Jesus the Christ is false!
4. Any other God but YAHWEH is false!
5. That another deity is equal to or greater than YAHWEH is false!

1 John 4:3
And every spirit that confesseth not that Jesus Christ is come in the flesh is not of God: and this is that spirit of antichrist, whereof ye have heard that it should come; and even now already is it in the world.

2 Corinthians 11:4
For if he that cometh preacheth another Jesus, whom we have not preached, or if ye receive another spirit, which ye have not received, or another gospel, which ye have not accepted, ye might well bear with him.

Galatians 1:8
But though we, or an angel from heaven, preach any other gospel unto you than that which we have preached unto you, let him be accursed.

False doctrine is oftentimes a product of:
- rebellion against God
- the mixing of what is sacred with what is profane
- ungodly relationships
- religious feuds
- over-emphasis on a set of scriptures
- biblical misinterpretation

Rebellion Against God

Lucifer made a decision to rebel against God, but why? He wanted to be equal to or greater than God. Isaiah 14:12-14 confirms this; it reads, "How art thou fallen from heaven, O Lucifer, son of the morning! how art thou cut down to the ground, which didst weaken the nations! For thou hast said in thine heart, I will ascend into heaven, I will exalt my throne above the stars of God: I will sit also upon the mount of the congregation, in the sides of the north: I will ascend above the heights of the clouds; I will be like the most High." What were the stars of God? The angels, of course. Remember the arrangements of the Heavens.

First Heaven	Second Heaven	Third Heaven
Atmosphere Above Earth	Sun, Moon and Stars	God's Abode

The Second Heaven is where God's angels are. What's above the stars of God? The Third Heaven, which again is God's abode! So, Lucifer literally planned to leave his position and elevate himself to a higher role! The seed started in his mind, and eventually, he acted upon it. He fashioned a weapon called a lie and used it to bewitch one-third of God's angels. Revelation 12:3-4 reads, "And there appeared another wonder in heaven; and behold a great red dragon, having seven heads and ten horns, and seven crowns upon his heads. And his tail drew the third part of the stars of heaven, and did cast them to the earth." The third part of the stars in Heaven were angels! When Lucifer lied to them, he essentially created what we now call false doctrine! He was cast into the Earth, and he then took his false doctrine and made his way into the Garden of Eden, where he found Eve. He advertised his lies to her and she bought into them! When Eve took a bite of the forbidden fruit, she rebelled against God! Hear me—she'd rebelled against God the minute she considered Satan's lies and the moment she touched that fruit! 1 Samuel 15:23 says, "For rebellion is as the sin of witchcraft, and stubbornness is as iniquity and idolatry."

Nowadays, we still have people rebelling against God and creating false doctrines, meaning, they know the truth and they know that what they are promoting is false, nevertheless, their insatiable appetites for fame, wealth and notoriety are almost unquenchable! Somewhere on their journey in Christ, they got offended or they allowed jealousy, envy and comparison to tempt them into sin. From there, they began their campaigns against Heaven. This is how many (if not most) false religions were started!

The Mixing of What is Sacred with What is Profane

1 John 2:15-16

Love not the world, neither the things that are in the world. If any man love the world, the love of the Father is not in him. For all that is in the world, the lust of the flesh, and the lust of the eyes, and the pride of life, is not of the Father, but is of the world.

Most of us have served our time in the world, and we came to love much of what the world had to offer, regardless of how profane and perverse it was! So, when we came to Christ, we brought many of our desires, habits and strongholds with us. Eventually, as we grew in Christ, we allowed the scent of the world to dissipate and our appetite for worldly things to pass away. For many of us, this was no easy transition, but we made it! But what happens when a believer loves the world so much that he or she refuses to let it go? That believer becomes what the Bible refers to as "double-minded." God refers to these types of believers as adulterers. In James 4:4, He goes on record saying, "Ye adulterers and adulteresses, know ye not that the friendship of the world is enmity with God? Whosoever therefore will be a friend of the world is the enemy of God." In Matthew 6:24, Jesus dealt with double-mindedness; He said, "No man can serve two masters: for either he will hate the one, and love the other; or else he will hold to the one, and despise the other. Ye cannot serve God and mammon." Nevertheless, as this world grows more and more perverse, we see an uprising of believers attempting to mix worldly doctrines with the Word, not realizing that Jesus (once again) is the Living Word of God, therefore, anything that is contrary to who He is, He will vomit it out! In Revelation 3:15-

16, He rebuked the Church of Laodicea with these words, "I know thy works, that thou art neither cold nor hot: I would thou wert cold or hot. So then because thou art lukewarm, and neither cold nor hot, I will spue thee out of my mouth."

Mixture is oftentimes the product of salvation with no sanctification. There has to be a gap between us getting saved and us attempting to minister to others. Within this span of time, we should be focusing on growing our relationship with the Most High God and removing the plank, speck or mote from our own eyes. In other words, we should be focusing on our own deliverance. When there is no space for sanctification, mixture is inevitable! Mark 2:22 gives us a picture of what this looks like; it reads, "And no man putteth new wine into old bottles: else the new wine doth burst the bottles, and the wine is spilled, and the bottles will be marred: but new wine must be put into new bottles."

Ungodly Relationships

Ungodly relationships can be familial, platonic or romantic, and unfortunately, there are many believers on Earth who put their family, their friends, their lovers and themselves before God! The problem isn't that these people don't love God; the problem is they love something or someone more than they love God! This means that love comes in measures, and anytime we love a thing or a person more than we love God, we have made that thing or person an idol in our lives.

Matthew 10:37
He that loveth father or mother more than me is not worthy of me: and he that loveth son or daughter more than me is not worthy of me.

Every believer goes through stages of maturity, and all too often, when the believer is still what the Bible refers to as a "babe in Christ," that believer will find himself or herself in a relationship with someone who does not have God's heart. It is not uncommon to see believers walk away from the faith, walk away from their churches and to completely sabotage Kingdom relationships in their attempts to build relationships with their lovers. And get this—many of these believers are truly anointed! Some of them are Apostles, some are Prophets, some are Pastors, Evangelists and Teachers! As a matter of fact, we witnessed the Teacher nearly go extinct because many of them became distracted by the enemy when they were yet still students! In short, they awakened love before its time, and what's more is, they awakened it with someone who did not have God's heart! Nevertheless, because they are determined to preach the gospel or prove themselves to themselves, many of them created doctrines that would support their lifestyles. Thankfully, many of these doctrines never see the light of day, but many doctrines established on the foundations of rejection, abandonment and hurt are circulating amongst the masses today! They promote retribution more than they promote God!

Two notable kings in the Bible fell into this very trap; they are:
1. King Ahab
2. King Solomon

And in both of these cases, the women successfully turned the kings' hearts away from God and, of course, both kings attempted to mix that which was unholy with that which was holy. It didn't work! Instead, both men paid a very notable price for their rebellion and their double-mindedness! And of course, they weren't the only men in the Bible who intermarried with pagan worshipers. YAHWEH strictly forbade this practice because it always led to mixture, and mixture will always lead to the establishment of false doctrine.

Religious Feuds

1 Corinthians 1:10-13

Now I beseech you, brethren, by the name of our Lord Jesus Christ, that ye all speak the same thing, and that there be no divisions among you; but that ye be perfectly joined together in the same mind and in the same judgment. For it hath been declared unto me of you, my brethren, by them which are of the house of Chloe, that there are contentions among you. Now this I say, that every one of you saith, I am of Paul; and I of Apollos; and I of Cephas; and I of Christ. Is Christ divided? was Paul crucified for you? or were ye baptized in the name of Paul?

In the aforementioned text, we see two phenomena about to take place:
1. The splitting of the church
2. The emergence of denominations

Thankfully, Apostle Paul was able to intercept this division before it continued to spread. What's amazing is—oftentimes denominational splits are the result of two or more immature believers who place emphasis on shallow facts. For example, some of the believers at the Church of Corinth began to distinguish themselves from their brethren; some of them said, "I was baptized by Paul," while others boasted about being baptized by Cephas (Peter). This is exactly how denominational splits occur! They are established on shallow grounds! This is why Jesus said in Mark 3:25, "And if a house be divided against itself, that house cannot stand."

Another notable split took place in England in the 16th century as a result of a feud between

King Henry VIII and Pope Clement VII. The adulterous king wanted to divorce his wife, Catherine of Aragon, because:

1. She had not produced for him a male heir. At that time in history, it was largely believed that women determined the gender of a child.
2. He wanted to marry Anne Bolelyn. He'd attempted to have an affair with her, but when she'd refused his advances, he became even more anxious to divorce his wife so that he could marry Anne.

During that time, the only church in England was the Roman Catholic Church, and the Roman Catholic Church simply did not allow divorces. The Church, at that time, was the ruling authority. Determined to divorce his wife, King Henry VIII tried to appeal to the church, and when this was ineffective, he created his own church by removing the Catholic Church from papal authority. Also known as papal supremacy or papacy, papal authority is "the office and jurisdiction of the bishop of Rome, the pope (Latin papa, from Greek pappas, "father"), who presides over the central government of the Roman Catholic Church, the largest of the three major branches of Christianity" (Encyclopedia Britannica). This split is known as the English Reformation, and as a result of that split, the king created the Church of England and appointed himself as Supreme Head of the Church of England. This allowed him to annul his marriage to Queen Anne and subject biblical interpretation to his own desires.

There have been many religious feuds driven by personal greed, lust and ambition. These feuds have caused many denominational splits, and there has always been people who have pledged allegiance to one side of each feud. And when this happens, the leaders on one or both sides of the split oftentimes feel the need to distinguish their religion from their opposer's religion. When this happens, false doctrine is born.

Over-Emphasis on a Set of Scriptures

Many religions and Christian denominations were built on the over-emphasis of a particular scripture. Their doctrines were not built on "the" Word of God, but rather "a" word from God. This is why you'll notice that some religions are very dogmatic, stubborn and constricting. What they often promote as dedication is nothing but a commitment to a set of principles and works that they feel they must do in order to please God or to pacify His wrath. This is what we often refer to as heresy.

Here's the truth—in many faiths and denominations, you will find truths and facts that are not always promoted, highlighted or emphasizied in other religious sects, and this has easily become the foundation by which many false religions establish themselves. All the same, because they are false religions, their biblical interpretations are peppered with falsehoods. For example, there are some religions that center their doctrines around the way women dress; these religions use fear, lies and biblical misinterpretation, whether intentional or unintentional, to oppress and control women. They will often misuse or misinterpret scriptures like Apostle Paul's letter to Timothy regarding women in the church. It reads, "But I suffer not a woman to teach, nor to usurp authority over the man, but to be in silence" (1 Timothy 2:12). Because of the misinterpretation or, better yet, misunderstanding of this scripture, many false doctrines have been created that are used to muzzle and manipulate women. This is unfortunate because God said in Acts 2:17-18, "And it shall come to pass in the last days, saith God, I will pour out of my Spirit upon all flesh: and your sons and your daughters shall prophesy, and your young men shall see visions, and your old men shall dream dreams: And on my servants and on my handmaidens I will pour out in those days of my Spirit; and they shall prophesy." But why would Apostle Paul say that a woman shouldn't teach? First and foremost, we must understand that Apostle Paul did not have the authority to establish new laws. As an apostle of God, his assignment was to preach, promote and demonstrate the Kingdom of God! This doesn't mean that he was in error; it simply means that what Apostle Paul said was not a new commandment; it was not the establishment of new doctrine! It is important to understand context and history when reading scriptures. Apostle Paul was dealing with an issue that was prevalent at that time. His letters were to specific churches, and he would often address issues of perversion and rebellion that were commonplace in those particular regions. For example, in 1 Corinthians 5:5, we witness the apostle instructing the Church at Corinth regarding a rumor he'd heard. He'd discovered that there were men in the Corinthian Church who had been engaging in sexual affairs with their stepmothers! What did he tell the church to do regarding this matter? He said for them to "turn over such a one to Satan." How hard of a charge is this?! Nevertheless, have you noticed that most heretics who overemphasize Apostle Paul's charge to not allow women to teach never seem to promote this particular scripture? What about Apostle Paul's charge for men to not pray with their heads covered? He also mentioned that it was a shame for a man to have long hair. Why are these words not established as doctrinal beliefs in many religions? The reason for this is, in heretic faiths, men often place emphasis on the scriptures that would allow them to have the lives and lifestyles that they want; this is because it gives them a false sense of security. Many of these men wrestle with rejection, fear of rejection, abandonment and fear of abandonment. By establishing doctrines that demoralize and castigate women, they essentially secure their positions in the lives of the women who turn to them for answers. This allows their perversion to be as expressive as it wants to be without being questioned or challenged. You'll notice that many false faiths allow men to have multiple wives, and if they are not allowed to have multiple wives, their sexual indiscretions are oftentimes swept under the rug, while their wives are encouraged to remain silent, supportive and submissive.

Heresy

"doctrine or opinion at variance with established standards" (or, as Johnson defines it, "an opinion of private men different from that of the catholick and orthodox church"), c. 1200, from Old French heresie, eresie "heresy," and by extension "sodomy, immorality" (12c.), from Latin hæresis, "school of thought, philosophical sect." The Latin word is from Greek hairesis "a taking or choosing for oneself, a choice, a means of taking; a deliberate plan, purpose; philosophical sect, school," from haireisthai "take, seize," middle voice of hairein "to choose," a word of unknown origin, perhaps cognate with Hittite šaru "booty," Welsh herw "booty;" but Beekes offers "no etymology."

The Greek word was used by Church writers in reference to various sects, schools, etc. in the New Testament: the Sadducees, the Pharisees, and even the Christians, as sects of Judaism. Hence the meaning "unorthodox religious sect or doctrine" in the Latin word as used by Christian writers in Late Latin. But in English bibles it usually is translated sect. Transferred (non-religious) use in English is from late 14c.

Source: Online Etymology Dictionary

Heretic

"one who holds a doctrine at variance with established or dominant standards," mid-14c., from Old French eretique (14c., Modern French hérétique), from Church Latin haereticus "of or belonging to a heresy," as a noun, "a heretic," from Greek hairetikos "able to choose" (in the New Testament, "heretical"), verbal adjective of hairein "to take" (see heresy).

[T]he heretic is not an unbeliever (far from it) but rather a man who emphasizes some point of doctrine too strongly and obsessively. [Russell Kirk, "T.S. Eliot and his Age"]

Source: Online Etymology Dictionary

Biblical Misinterpretation

1 Corinthians 2:14

But the natural man receiveth not the things of the Spirit of God: for they are foolishness unto him: neither can he know them, because they are spiritually discerned.

2 Peter 1:20

Knowing this first, that no prophecy of the scripture is of any private interpretation.

There's no getting around it—we need God's Spirit to interpret the scriptures, otherwise, we'll take the black and white letters on a page and run them through our personal filters of experience, fear, religion and perversion, and what would be birthed from us would be called heresy. Hear me—if the Bible tells us to "rightly divide" the Word of Truth, this means that it is possible to wrongly divide the Word. Wrongly dividing the Word is called dismemberment; this is when a person attempts to eat one part of Jesus' flesh, all the while, ignoring the other parts.

Biblical misinterpretation is the product of a believer or an unbeliever attempting to understand the scriptures using his or her own intellect and, in many cases, biblical misinterpretation is the result of a believer being legalistic. Legalism is oftentimes the product of fear, false religions, fear-based religions and personal agendas. Proverbs 3:5-6 reads, "Trust in the LORD with all thine heart; and lean not unto thine own understanding. In all thy ways acknowledge him, and he shall direct thy paths."

Heresy

This week we begin a two part study of the word αἵρεσις (Strong's #139) which means "heresy" or even the name of a "religious sect." Αἵρεσις comes from the verb αἱρέω, "to take," or "remove." Only the middle voice of this verb (αἱρέομαι, Strong's #138) is found in the New Testament. Αἱρέομαι means "to choose, to elect, to prefer." This basic meaning of "to choose" is an important element in understanding the meaning behind "heresy."
In Classical Greek, αἵρεσις has two meanings. The first is "to take," or "remove." The second is "choice," or "selection." Αἵρεσις not only represents the choice, but also the "sect," or "group" which results from the choice.
Αἵρεσις is found five times in the Old Testament Greek Septuagint. The most notable are two instances found in Leviticus representing the "freewill offering" (choice) and another in Nehemiah where it is used to denote the two "sections" (groups) of the choir.

Source: StudyLight.org

Notice in the aforementioned definition, the Greek word for "heresy" (hairesis) means "to remove." Religious sects do just that! They remove or ignore certain scriptures, all the while, highlighting and placing emphasis on other scriptures. This is where the confusion come from! They are oftentimes able to point out some truths; this is what gives off the magnetic effect and draws people to them, but they use those truths to gain access to one of the most sacred compartments in a believer's mind; that compartment is called trust! Trust is the password to the heart.

HOW TO JUDGE PROPHECY

Let's go back to the Garden of Eden. In Genesis 3, we find Satan being judged once again, but this time for his role in deceiving Eve. Genesis 3:15 reads, "And the LORD God said unto the serpent, Because thou hast done this, thou art cursed above all cattle, and above every beast of the field; upon thy belly shalt thou go, and dust shalt thou eat all the days of thy life: And I will put enmity between thee and the woman, and between thy seed and her seed; it shall bruise thy head, and thou shalt bruise his heel." What seed was He referring to? The answer can be found in Revelations 12:13-17 which reads, "And when the dragon saw that he was cast unto the earth, he persecuted the woman which brought forth the man child. And to the woman were given two wings of a great eagle, that she might fly into the wilderness, into her place, where she is nourished for a time, and times, and half a time, from the face of the serpent. And the serpent cast out of his mouth water as a flood after the woman, that he might cause her to be carried away of the flood. And the earth helped the woman, and the earth opened her mouth, and swallowed up the flood which the dragon cast out of his mouth. And the dragon was wroth with the woman, and went to make war with the remnant of her seed, which keep the commandments of God, and have the testimony of Jesus Christ." What God released while judging Satan was a prophetic word. Who is Jesus Christ? He is the literal Word of God! He is the Way, the Truth and the Life! This is why the moment Satan heard those words, his heart melted within him. It is impossible for God to lie, and Satan knows this! Therefore, he decided to wage war against Jesus and those who would accept Him as their Lord and Savior. But he couldn't wage war against the Word of God and win, so he declared war against the words of God (you and I).

John 10:34
Jesus answered them, Is it not written in your law, I said, Ye are gods?

We are all members of the body of Christ; Christ is the Word of God. We are words; this is why we cannot afford to be divided. When we all come together, we create an atmosphere for Jesus to manifest Himself, but only to the degree of our unity. This is why the scriptures tell us that we prophesy in part! This is also why the Bible warns us that a house divided cannot stand! Satan knows this so what he's done is weaponized ignorance, trauma and ambition, and he uses these weapons to divide God's church! He can't stop God's Word from coming to pass, so his goal now is to delay his own destruction. How does he do this? He went to make war with the remnant of the woman's seed. But hear me—war and warfare don't always look like guns, bombs, swords, tear gas and rocket launchers! Oftentimes, the most effective traps are designed to appeal to our dissatisfaction! How would you trap a mouse in your house? Would you shoot at it? Would you brandish a sword? No. The most effective way to take down that mouse is to appeal to its hunger. You'd place cheese in a rat trap, set the trap in an area that the mouse frequents and you'd steer clear of that area so that you can give the mouse a false sense of security. Driven by its own hunger, the mouse will eventually go into the trap. If Satan disguises himself as an angel of light, please understand that he also disguises himself as whatever it is that you want the most! Why is this? Again, you are a word of God; you are a prophecy that has come to pass. We prophesy in part, so when you come together in unity and harmony with other believers, you manifest the person of Jesus Christ!

With that being said, how do you judge prophecy? In truth, we've had it wrong for many years! We've tried to "discern" prophecies using the perverted filters of our understanding! We've looked for God to manifest His words through men and women with titles, oftentimes ignoring our sons, daughters and the old men that God speaks about in Acts 2:17-18. But before we go any further. Let's look up the word "prophecy."

Prophecy
c. 1200, prophecie, prophesie, "the function of a prophet; inspired utterance; the prediction of future events," from Old French profecie (12c. Modern French prophétie) and directly from Late Latin prophetia, in Medieval Latin also prophecia (source also of Spanish profecia, Italian profezia), from Greek prophēteia "gift of interpreting the will of the gods," from prophētēs (see prophet). Meaning "thing spoken or written by a prophet" is from late 13c.
Online Etymology Dictionary

Prophesy
"speak by divine inspiration, foretell future events," mid-14c., prophecein, prophesein, from Old French profeciier, prophecier (13c.), from prophecie (see prophecy). The noun and verb spellings were not fully differentiated until 18c. Related: Prophesied; prophesying. Other verb forms in Middle English were prophetise (mid-14c., from Old French profetisier and Latin prophetizare), prophet (mid-15c.).
Online Etymology Dictionary

Judging Prophets

Greek	Hebrew
Prophéteia	Naba
prophecy, prophesying; the gift of communicating and enforcing revealed truth.	speak (or sing) by inspiration (in prediction or simple discourse):—prophesy(-ing), make self a prophet.
Strong's Concordance	Blue Letter Bible

Here's what we're not often taught. We are instruments of the Most High God, much like Lucifer was! God uses our mouths and our bodies to prophesy. But here's where things get slippery! Does God possess us so that we can prophesy? He can if He chooses, but God prefers to use yielded vessels! In other words, He often uses words that are in alignment with His Word! Why is this? Because we don't just prophesy; prophecy isn't God invading our intellect, causing our eyes to roll into the back of our heads and move around eerily! Prophecy is not just us speaking what thus saith the Lord, but prophecy is us becoming what God said! If we understand this, it becomes easier to judge prophecy by doing what religion has taught us not to do—judge one another! But first and foremost, let's acknowledge this truth—the gifts and the callings are without repentance! God can use whomsoever He chooses to use, regardless of whether that person is submitted to Him or in direct opposition of Him. This is why you shouldn't completely dismiss someone whose lifestyle doesn't necessarily reflect God. However, you can and you should judge the words that they speak (we'll discuss this shortly). Whenever you come across a believer who prophesies, understand this—that believer prophesies more with his or her choices than the believer does with his or her words!

Matthew 7:15-20

Beware of false prophets, which come to you in sheep's clothing, but inwardly they are ravening wolves. Ye shall know them by their fruits. Do men gather grapes of thorns, or figs of thistles? Even so every good tree bringeth forth good fruit; but a corrupt tree bringeth forth evil fruit. A good tree cannot bring forth evil fruit, neither can a corrupt tree bring forth good fruit. Every tree that bringeth not forth good fruit is hewn down, and cast into the fire. Wherefore by their fruits ye shall know them.

But wait? What are the fruits that we should be measuring? Galatians 5:22-24 answers this question for us! It reads, "But the fruit of the Spirit is love, joy, peace, longsuffering, gentleness, goodness, faith, meekness, temperance: against such there is no law. And they that are

Christ's have crucified the flesh with the affections and lusts." For example, if and whenever you see pride, don't trust the words coming from the vessel who is prophesying! After all, the scriptures tell us that God resists the proud and gives grace to the humble! What this means is that while God may occasionally use an ass (see Numbers 22:21-39), those are oftentimes rare occurrences that happen because there's no prophet or yielded vessel in a particular locale for God to use. Nevertheless, every prophet and prophetic person will tell you whether they are false or not through their lifestyles and their choices! And hear me—this doesn't mean that we have to be perfect to be used by God, what it means is that we must be intentional and we must yield ourselves to Him! If a prophet or prophetic person yields his or her body to sin, that person's words cannot be trusted. Why is that? Because that individual isn't just a mouthpiece of God, but his or her choices reflect whether or not he or she trusts in God! So, if the works of the flesh are prevalent in that individual's life, it's because the person in question does not fully trust God, and if he or she doesn't trust God, how can the individual truly know that what he or she is sensing is from God?! Remember, Satan does disguise himself as an angel of light!

But aren't we supposed to refrain from judging others? Absolutely not! The Bible gives us clear instructions regarding measuring the fruits of another human being!

Measuring Fruits

	Scripture	Scriptural Text	Summary
1	Matthew 7:1-5	Judge not, that ye be not judged. For with what judgment ye judge, ye shall be judged: and with what measure ye mete, it shall be measured to you again. And why beholdest thou the mote that is in thy brother's eye, but considerest not the beam that is in thine own eye? Or how wilt thou say to thy brother, Let me pull out the mote out of thine eye; and, behold, a beam is in thine own eye? Thou hypocrite, first cast out the beam out of thine own eye; and then shalt thou see clearly to cast out the mote out of thy brother's eye.	In this, the Lord is NOT telling us that we cannot judge others; this scripture is literally about hypocrisy! In other words, don't judge someone else when you're struggling with the same issue! For example, don't stand on the front of a picket line protesting homosexuality if you're in fornication! It's hypocrisy! You can't judge someone else's sin just because it doesn't look like yours! But once you have defeated your own demons, you can then go and cast those same demons out of someone else!

2	Galatians 5:16-18	This I say then, Walk in the Spirit, and ye shall not fulfill the lust of the flesh. For the flesh lusteth against the Spirit, and the Spirit against the flesh: and these are contrary the one to the other: so that ye cannot do the things that ye would. But if ye be led of the Spirit, ye are not under the law.	This scripture is all about self-control! In short, because you are a spirit wrapped in flesh, you will feel lust rising up in your flesh; this is normal! But don't give into those desires; instead, overcome those desires by crucifying your flesh every day!
3	1 John 4:1	Beloved, believe not every spirit, but try the spirits whether they are of God: because many false prophets are gone out into the world.	Another word for "try" is "trial" or "test." To put a spirit on trial, you must interrogate it with the Word of God. This requires the fruit of patience! This means that you need to know the Word and then measure that spirit against the Word. If it's not from God, it will begin to manifest.
4	John 7:24	Judge not according to the appearance, but judge righteous judgment.	Don't be moved by what you see; don't allow your carnality to pervert your judgment! Judge a thing in accordance with the Word of God, not your opinion!
5	James 4:7	Submit yourselves therefore to God. Resist the devil, and he will flee from you.	In short, resist whatever temptation you are faced with! Consider Jesus' temptation in the wilderness. He continued to speak the Word because He is the Word! And what happened when it was over? Satan fled!

You'll notice that the aforementioned pointers don't point too much away from you, but are mainly centered around making sure that your heart is in alignment with God's heart! Whenever we focus on someone else's gardens, we leave our own gardens open, unattended and susceptible to an attack. Hear me—your garden is your heart! This is where you grow the fruits of the Spirit; this is also where you defeat the works of the flesh!

Proverbs 4:23
Keep thy heart with all diligence; for out of it *are* the issues of life.

Proverbs 25:28
He that hath no rule over his own spirit is like a city that is broken down, and without walls.

Fruits of the Spirit		
Love	Joy	Peace
Longsuffering	Gentleness	Goodness
Faith	Meekness	Temperance

Works of the Flesh		
Adultery	Fornication	Uncleanness
Lasciviousness	Idolatry	Witchcraft
Hatred	Variance	Emulations
Wrath	Strife	Sedition
Heresies	Envyings	Murders
Drunkenness		Revelings

Judging Prophecies

How do you judge prophecy? First and foremost, it doesn't matter who delivers a word to you, you must first test it to make sure that it's from God. It's important to note that even real prophets can be deceived by Satan. We've witnessed a lot over the last few years with so many prophets and prophetic voices rushing to the forefront to deliver what they've packaged as prophetic words about anything from the Super Bowl to the presidential election, and many of them were publicly humiliated when those words did not come to pass! Were they all false prophets? Some were; others were not. Howbeit, the true prophets had a moment much like the moment when Milcaiah was brought before Ahab to prophesy. In that moment, he was told to align his words with the words of Jezebel's prophets. In a moment of sarcasm, he did just that; that is, until Ahab made him swear to tell the truth. The difference is, however, that many prophets and prophetic voices today are not being told what to say; rather, they feel pressured to parrot what they hear other noteworthy leaders saying. So, they take a gamble and record videos of themselves releasing false prophecies; they then allow their fingers to hover over the "publish" button until they finally get enough courage to push it. And with the push of a finger, their credibility is completely shattered. Again, this is why every word should be tested! Yes, even if it's a word that you want!

We prophesy in part. Let's reestablish this! We are all members of the body of Christ. Think about limbs. You may come in contact with someone who claims to be a kneecap when you are a knee, but for whatever reason, the two of you are not in sync with one another! That person may attempt to prophesy to you, but you have to measure how well it connects with you. If it is not in sync with what God has spoken to you, it may be:
1. False.
2. Out of Season (the person released it too soon).
3. Misinterpreted (you or the person misunderstood what God was trying to say).

To measure a prophetic word, ask yourself the following questions:
1. Does it line up with scripture?
2. Do you sense the witness of the Holy Spirit in relation to that word?
3. Does your spirit bear witness with the prophetic word?
4. Is the person prophesying in love, meekness or humility, or is the prophecy being delivered through the filters of pride, arrogance, offense, comparison or envy?
5. Who does the word glorify—God or the prophetic voice giving it?
6. Where was the word delivered? Did the person catch you in the parking lot of your church or in the foyer? Hear me—prophetic words given out of order are oftentimes false or demonic!
7. Did the person ask for money before giving that word? Hear me—there is a big difference between a prophet and a profit!
8. Does that word draw you closer to God or drive you further away from Him?

Another way to judge prophecy is:
1. Get your witnesses together. Out of the mouths of two or three witnesses, a thing is established! Take it to your church's leadership and ask them to examine the word and pray over it.
2. Wait it out! Don't try to make it come to pass! Just lay it before the Lord in prayer and wait it out!
3. Stay in the will of God. The objective of a false word is to drive you into sin or into error! Don't leave your position; stay in God's will!

Other Prophetic Facts to Consider

1. Just because someone prophesies does not mean that the person in question is a

prophet (see Acts 2:17).
2. Prophecies are not subject to our own interpretation (see 2 Peter 1:20).
3. (Reminder) We prophesy in part (1 Corinthians 13:9)!
4. Prophecy is given to edify, exhort and comfort (see 1 Corinthians 14:3).
5. God resists the proud and gives grace to the humble. A proud prophet is a false one (James 4:6)!
6. Two or three prophets should speak, and the others should weigh what they've said (see 1 Corinthians 14:29).
7. The spirits of the prophets are subject to other prophets. Any prophet who refuses to stand in the company of other prophets and submit their words to them should not be trusted (1 Corinthians 14:32).

Gifts of the Spirit

Word of Wisdom
Word of Knowledge
Faith
Gifts of Healing
Working of Miracles
Prophecies
Discerning of Spirits
Diverse Tongues
Interpretation of Tongues

Scriptures About False Prophets

The following scriptures were taken from the ESV Bible

Deuteronomy 13:1-5

"If a prophet or a dreamer of dreams arises among you and gives you a sign or a wonder, and the sign or wonder that he tells you comes to pass, and if he says, 'Let us go after other gods,' which you have not known, 'and let us serve them,' you shall not listen to the words of that prophet or that dreamer of dreams. For the Lord your God is testing you, to know whether you love the Lord your God with all your heart and with all your soul. You shall walk after the Lord your God and fear him and keep his commandments and obey his voice, and you shall serve him and hold fast to him. But that prophet or that dreamer of dreams shall be put to death, because he has taught rebellion against the Lord your God, who brought you out of the land of Egypt and redeemed you out of the house of slavery, to make you leave the way in which the Lord your God commanded you to walk. So you shall purge the evil from your midst.

Matthew 7:15-16

Beware of false prophets, who come to you in sheep's clothing but inwardly are ravenous wolves. You will recognize them by their fruits. Are grapes gathered from thornbushes, or figs from thistles?

Matthew 24:11

And many false prophets will arise and lead many astray.

Matthew 24:24

For false christs and false prophets will arise and perform great signs and wonders, so as to lead astray, if possible, even the elect.

2 Timothy 4:3-4

For the time is coming when people will not endure sound teaching, but having itching ears they will accumulate for themselves teachers to suit their own passions, and will turn away from listening to the truth and wander off into myths.

2 Peter 2:1-3

But false prophets also arose among the people, just as there will be false teachers among you, who will secretly bring in destructive heresies, even denying the Master who bought them, bringing upon themselves swift destruction. And many will follow their sensuality, and because of them the way of truth will be blasphemed. And in their greed they will exploit you with false words. Their condemnation from long ago is not idle, and their destruction is not asleep.

Ezekiel 13:9

My hand will be against the prophets who see false visions and who give lying divinations. They shall not be in the council of my people, nor be enrolled in the register of the house of Israel, nor shall they enter the land of Israel. And you shall know that I am the Lord God.

1 John 4:1

Beloved, do not believe every spirit, but test the spirits to see whether they are from God, for many false prophets have gone out into the world.

2 Timothy 4:3

For the time is coming when people will not endure sound teaching, but having itching ears they will accumulate for themselves teachers to suit their own passions,

Major and Minor Prophets in the Bible

Major Prophets (List)

Isaiah	Jeremiah
Ezekiel	Daniel

Minor Prophets (List)

Hosea	Joel
Amos	Obadiah
Jonah	Micah
Nahum	Habakkuk
Zephaniah	Haggai
Zechariah	Malachi

Other Notable Prophets in the Bible

Adam	Moses
Noah	Abraham
Joshua	Samuel
David	Deborah
Joseph	Elijah
Job	Jacob

Complete List of Biblical Prophets

Aaron	Abel	Abraham	Agabus
Agur	Ahab	Ahijah	Amos
Anna	Asaph	Azariah	Azur
Barnabas	Daniel	David	Deborah

Eldad	Eliezer	Elihu	Elijah
Elisabeth (mother of John the Baptist)	Elisha	Enoch	Ezekiel
Gad	Habakkuk	Haggai	Hanani
Hananiah	Hosea	Huldah	Iddo
Isaac	Isaiah	Jacob	Jahaziel
Jehu	Jeremiah	Jesus	Job
Joel	John of Patmos	John the Baptist	Jonah
Joseph	Joseph (secondary father of Jesus)	Joshua	Judas Barsabbas
King Nebuchadnezzar	King Solomon	Lucius of Cyrene	Malachi
Manaen	Mary (mother of Jesus)	Medad	Micah
Micaiah	Miriam	Moses	Nahum
Nathan	Noadiah	Noah	Obadiah
Oded	Philip the Evangelist	Samuel	Shemaiah
Silas	Simeon Niger	Simeon of Jerusalem	The four daughters of Philip the Evangelist
The seventy elders of Israel	Two Witnesses	Urijah	Zechariah (father of John the Baptist)
Zechariah (son of Berechiah)	Zechariah (son of Jehoiada)	Zedekiah	Zephaniah

PROPHET

| Seer | Oracle | Mediator |
| Prognosticator | Forecaster | Predictor |

IDENTIFICATION OF AND DELIVERANCE FROM CULTS

Mass Suicide at Jonestown

On November 18, 1978, Peoples Temple, founder, Jim Jones leads hundreds of his followers in a mass murder-suicide at their agricultural commune in a remote part of the South American nation of Guyana. Many of Jones' followers willingly ingested a poison-laced punch while others were forced to do so at gunpoint. The final death toll at Jonestown that day was 909; a third of those who perished were children.

Jim Jones was a charismatic churchman who established the Peoples Temple, a Christian sect, in Indianapolis in the 1950s. He preached against racism, and his integrated congregation attracted many African Americans. In 1965, he moved the group to Northern California, settling in Ukiah after 1971 in San Francisco. In the 1970s, his church was accused by the media of financial fraud, physical abuse of its members, and mistreatment of children. In response to the mounting criticism, the increasingly paranoid Jones invited his congregation to move with him to Guyana, where he promised they would build a socialist utopia. Three years earlier, a small group of his followers had traveled to the tiny nation to set up what would become Jonestown on a tract of jungle.

Jonestown did not turn out to be the paradise their leader had promised. Temple members worked long days in the fields and were subjected to harsh punishments if they questioned Jones' authority. Their passports were confiscated, their letters home were censored, members were encouraged to inform on one another and forced to attend lengthy, late-night meetings. Jones, by then in declining mental health and addicted to drugs, was convinced the U.S. government and others were out to destroy him. He required Temple members to participate in mock suicide drills in the middle of the night.

In 1978, a group of former Temple members and concerned relatives of current members convinced U.S. Congressman Leo Ryan, a Democrat of California, to travel to Jonestown and investigate the settlement. On November 17, 1978, Ryan arrived in Jonestown with a group of journalists and other observers. At first the visit went well, but the next day, as Ryan's delegation was about to leave, several Jonestown residents approached the group and asked them for passage out of Guyana. Jones became distressed at the defection of his followers, and one of Jones' lieutenants attacked Ryan with a knife. The congressman escaped from the incident unharmed, but Jones then ordered Ryan and his companions ambushed and killed at the airstrip as they attempted to leave. The congressman and four others were murdered as they boarded their charter planes.

> Back in Jonestown, Jones commanded everyone to gather in the main pavilion and commit what he termed a "revolutionary act." The youngest members of the Peoples Temple were the first to die, as parents and nurses used syringes to drop a potent mix of cyanide, sedatives, and powdered fruit juice into children's throats. Adults then lined up to drink the poison-laced concoction while armed guards surrounded the pavilion.
>
> When Guyanese officials arrived at the Jonestown compound the next day, they found it carpeted with hundreds of bodies. Many people had perished with their arms around each other. A few residents managed to escape into the jungle as the suicides took place, while at least several dozen more Peoples Temple members, including several of Jones' sons, survived because they were in another part of Guyana at the time.
>
> Source: History.com

The story of Jim Jones and his followers is one of the most sinister examples of the dangers of a cult and the powers it has over people. But, before we go any further, let us establish one thing—a cult and the occult are not one in the same. While they are both demonic, they are not the same. Let us look at their definitions for clarity.

Cult	Occult
<ul><li>A system of religious veneration and devotion directed toward a particular figure or object.</li><li>A relatively small group of people having religious beliefs or practices regarded by others as strange or sinister.</li><li>A misplaced or excessive admiration for a particular person or thing.</li></ul>	The word 'occult' comes from a Latin word for 'hidden.' It is a collection of beliefs and practices founded on the premise that humans can tap into a supernatural world. Once connected to this other realm, various rituals and special knowledge are used by those involved in the occult to allow a person to gain abilities and power they would otherwise not possess. These powers include controlling the nature world or other people. Biblically, the occult is any practice that tries to gain supernatural power, abilities, or knowledge apart from the creator God.
Source: Oxford Lexico	Source: BibleStudy.org

Going Inside the Mind of a Cult Leader

Narcissism. It is one of the trending terms of today because it gives language to what so many people have experienced within their families, their churches and their romantic relationships.

After spending years trying to help someone who is mentally unhealthy, most people conclude there is something else working behind the scenes of their deranged loved ones' minds. After all, no human being can possibly be that delusional, that angry, that controlling, that suspicious or that insecure; right? It is difficult, if not impossible, for a sane person to grasp or understand the mind of someone who is bordering insanity. Nevertheless, most of us have tried a few times before we realized our efforts were futile, to say the least. But what is narcissism?

Narcissistic Personality Disorder

Narcissistic personality disorder — one of several types of personality disorders — is a mental condition in which people have an inflated sense of their own importance, a deep need for excessive attention and admiration, troubled relationships, and a lack of empathy for others. But behind this mask of extreme confidence lies a fragile self-esteem that's vulnerable to the slightest criticism.

A narcissistic personality disorder causes problems in many areas of life, such as relationships, work, school, or financial affairs. People with narcissistic personality disorder may be generally unhappy and disappointed when they're not given the special favors or admiration, they believe they deserve. They may find their relationships unfulfilling, and others may not enjoy being around them.

Treatment for narcissistic personality disorder centers around talk therapy (psychotherapy).

Source: Mayo Clinic

The word "narcissism" originates from a Greek myth about a young deity who ultimately became infatuated with his own reflection, and while this story is fictional, it does give us some insight into how the Greeks saw this disease. In other words, while the term may be relatively new to us, narcissism has been around for thousands of years.

Narcissus

Narcissus was a hunter in Greek mythology, son of the river god Cephissus and the nymph Liriope. He was a very beautiful young man, and many fell in love with him. However, he only showed them disdain and contempt. One day, while he was hunting in the woods, the Oread nymph Echo spotted him and immediately fell for him. When Narcissus sensed that someone was following him, Echo eventually revealed herself and tried to hug him. However, he pushed her off and told her not to disturb him. Echo, in despair, roamed around the woods for the rest of her life, and wilted away until all it remained of her was an echo sound. Nemesis, the goddess of retribution and revenge, learned what had happened and decided to punish Narcissus for his behavior. She led him to a pool; there, the man saw his reflection in

> the water and fell in love with it. Although he did not realize in the beginning that it was just a reflection, when he understood it, he fell in despair that his love could not materialize and committed suicide.
>
> Source: GreekMythology.com

Why are we talking about narcissists and narcissism? Because this is the disease, demon and driving force behind most, if not all, cult leaders. Within the bowels of a cult leader's mind, you will oftentimes find:

Narcissism	Schizophrenia	Paranoia
Fear	Bitterness/Hatred	Entitlement
Lust and Perversion	Hurt and Deep Hurt	Murder/Suicide
Borderline Personality Disorder	Envy/Jealousy/Comparison	Witchcraft

Note: Many of the traits on this list are also classified as demonic spirits.

Other spirits you will find include, but are not limited to:

Jezebel Spirit	Rejection and Fear of Rejection	Vagabond Spirit
Leviathan Spirit	Abandonment and Fear of Abandonment	Antichrist Spirit
Mind Control Spirits	Religious Spirits	Control and Witchcraft

Imagine the cult leader's mind as a vehicle. The vehicle is encapsulated in pride, and the driving force behind the wheel is rejection. Hear me—most religious cult leaders grew up in toxic homes where either their fathers were absent, or if they were present, they were abusive or neglectful. For example, Jim Jones told his cult, "I didn't have any love given to me — I didn't know what the hell love was." Charles Manson's mother was both an alcoholic and a prostitute. Ironically enough, the same is true for serial killers; they often come from toxic and unstable families. This is to say that cult leaders are nothing but serial killers in the making; this is why so many of them have led their congregants to commit suicide. But why? Again, imagine the cult leaders' mind as a vehicle. What is behind the wheel of that vehicle, in most cases, is rejection. Rejection is one of Satan's favorite weapons and spirits because of its effectiveness. You see, when a child has been rejected by one or both parents, this creates a huge void in the child's soul. And hear me—rejection does not always equate to the absence of a parent. A child can live with both parents and still experience rejection if one or both parents are emotionally or spiritually detached from the child, or if (at least) one of the parents spends little to no one-on-one time bonding with the child. Again, this creates a void in the child's life that is nearly unquenchable. This void will ultimately become infected with fear, anger, resentment, fear of rejection, fear of abandonment and anything else Satan can squeeze into it. Now, do not get me wrong—many notable men and women of God have come from chaotic backgrounds as well. However, when they found themselves at a crossroads between serving the Lord and serving the enemy, they simply chose a different path. Howbeit, cult leaders and serial killers oftentimes crave revenge, not just on the parents who failed them, but on a society they believe rejected and bullied them. And one thing about rejection is, while it can be and often is fact-based, meaning, the person in question did experience it, what makes rejection so potent is the way some people internalize it. For example, a young woman who was raised in a two-parent household to healthy, working, and supportive parents can experience rejection and she may decide that while her experience was painful, her life will go on. A young woman whose parents have been physically or emotionally absent, on the other hand, may experience (for example) the rejection of a friend or the rejection of a lover, and for her, this rejection could signal the end of the world. This is because she has seen a pattern of rejection in her life, so-much-so that every encounter she has with rejection can and oftentimes will feel unbearable. This is because she is not just experiencing the rejection from a man or a friend, but she feels the entirety of her history with rejection at once, and this pain can be so intense, she may find herself practicing unhealthy and toxic behaviors to ensure that she never experiences this pain again. Now, imagine that this woman was leading a small Bible study with a few women who hung onto her every word, and she began to rely on these women for her sense of self-worth. She experiences a few women resigning from her group, not because they do not like her as a leader, but because it conflicts with their work schedules or because they are dealing with some personal issues they want to commit more time to resolving. The woman (let's call her Sherry) will likely decide that the women in question either do not like her or she may reason that they are jealous of her. Either way, she takes their resignations personally, and consequently, she begins to tighten her grip on the remaining women. This causes other women to leave, which essentially causes her rejection wound to grow more and more. In short, because she has experienced rejection and internalized it the wrong way, she will spend her life sabotaging relationships and causing people to reject her. This will cause her to become more narcissistic (self-centered and manipulative) and will cause her to spiral more and more out of control. This is how a cult leader's mind works!

Having experienced repeated rejections and abandonment, many would-be cult leaders begin to place a strong emphasis on loyalty and honor. And while these traits are necessary and should be taught, the cult leader in the making will make them the cornerstone of his ministry, organization or whatever it is he is leading. (I am using the pronoun "he," but we all understand that both men and women can be cult leaders). The cult leader will then begin to target the weak, the outcast, the rejected and the overlooked within the constructs of whatever organization he is working or serving in. This is because he knows, all too well, how desperate they are for acceptance and affirmation. And when they do what he wants them to do, he rewards them by causing them to feel accepted. When they disappoint him, on the other hand, he will then weaponize their love for him and use it against them. The more his influence grows, the more his appetite grows for power; his fear of rejection also begins to expand until it consumes his mind. This is when you will see the detachment phase; he will begin to detach himself from the organization or ministry he is partnering with. This normally occurs after they begin to question his leadership, his practices, and his doctrine. Having garnered a decent number of followers, he will then have a series of meetings with those followers to air his grievances. Once he has their support and their word that they will follow him should he chooses to break away, he then comes up with the bright idea of starting his own organization or ministerial sect, where he is leader and many of his followers can serve in leadership roles. They all agree, and not long after this, the detachment is complete. He has successfully launched his own cult, but his story does not end there. The fear of rejection will continue to consume him; this is what causes him to place an excessive amount of his energy and attention on loyalty. Most of his messages will then be centered around the people who betrayed him. He will point out failures they have experienced as a result of their betrayal and he will publicly praise the ones who have a consistent track record of loyalty. But, even these behaviors will prove to be pointless, as other people will walk away. Eventually, he will begin to reason with himself (and those closest to him) that the information he shared within the organization is not only top-secret, but it is sacred and should be heavily guarded. This is oftentimes when the spirit of murder enters the picture. He manages to convince some of his most loyal followers that the people who have left his organization or ministry are traitors who are worthy of death! At this stage, he is consumed with wrath and rejection so-much-so that he is willing to take the life of another human being to protect himself from ever experiencing that pain again.

50 Characteristics of a Cult

Galatians 1:6-10
I marvel that ye are so soon removed from him that called you into the grace of Christ unto another gospel: Which is not another; but there be some that trouble you, and would pervert the gospel of Christ. But though we, or an angel from heaven, preach any other gospel unto

you than that which we have preached unto you, let him be accursed. As we said before, so say I now again, If any man preach any other gospel unto you than that ye have received, let him be accursed. For do I now persuade men, or God? Or do I seek to please men? For if I yet pleased men, I should not be the servant of Christ.

Matthew 24:4-12

And Jesus answered and said unto them, Take heed that no man deceive you.
For many shall come in my name, saying, I am Christ; and shall deceive many. And ye shall hear of wars and rumors of wars: see that ye be not troubled: for all these things must come to pass, but the end is not yet. For nation shall rise against nation, and kingdom against kingdom: and there shall be famines, and pestilences, and earthquakes, in divers places. All these are the beginning of sorrows.
Then shall they deliver you up to be afflicted, and shall kill you: and ye shall be hated of all nations for my name's sake. And then shall many be offended, and shall betray one another, and shall hate one another. And many false prophets shall rise, and shall deceive many. And because iniquity shall abound, the love of many shall wax cold.

Let us look at some of the cults that have risen in the 21st century.

Children of God

Initially called Teens for Christ, Children of God was founded in 1968 by rogue preacher David Berg in Huntington Beach, California. Attracting young runaways and hippies, Berg preached a kind of worship that combined the ways of Jesus Christ with the free love movement of the '60s. Group living, zealous proselytizing, and isolated communes were all pillars of the Children of God church. Members, who amounted to 15,000 people across the world at its peak, didn't work and children didn't go to school. The COG didn't believe in the nuclear family, so children were grouped together and lived separately from their parents.
In the late 1970s, COG became notorious for the sexual practices that one of Berg's own daughters later described as "religious prostitution." Berg coined the term "flirty fishing," a sexual practice in which women would allegedly have sex with men to bring them into the cult. Berg promoted and encouraged the sexualization of children within the COG community. As Berg manipulated the COG family with his sadistic practices, members started leaving the community, including the families of actors Joaquin Phoenix and Rose McGowan, who both grew up in Children of God communes.
Former COG members began coming forward in the early '90s, describing an environment that permitted and encouraged the physical and sexual abuse of young children. Ricky Dupuy

appeared on a talk show in 1993 and revealed that he'd been ordered by the group to rape a 10-year-old. Dupuy later committed suicide, like many other members of the group, including Berg's son Ricky Rodriguez, who was sexually abused throughout his life by his father and the group.

Source: Cosmopolitan.com

Heaven's Gate

Founded by Marshall Applewhite and Bonnie Nettles in the 1970s, Heaven's Gate was an ascetic cult that had a complicated belief system involving aliens, spaceships, and an imminent "recycling" of the planet Earth. After Nettles died in 1985, Applewhite took the group to even further extremes, and in 1997, he began claiming that a spacecraft was following the Hale-Bopp comet; this spacecraft would carry the Heaven's Gate members to the next level of existence.

While living in a rented home in San Diego, Applewhite and 38 followers died by suicide by taking phenobarbital mixed with applesauce. They all wore the same uniform and Nike shoes and had $5.75 in their pockets. As of today, the Heaven's Gate website still exists and is maintained by two of the group's followers.

Source: Cosmopolitan.com

The Movement for the Restoration of the Ten Commandments of God

This sect formed in the Kanungu district of Uganda in the 1980s and taught its members that they had to follow the Ten Commandments in order to survive the apocalypse, which the leaders believed was coming in 2000. When January 1, 2000, passed without incident, members began to question why their leaders had failed to get their apocalypse date right and leaders then predicted that the real end would come on March 17. It did, but not because of anything supernatural—the leaders set fire to the Movement church, killing more than 500 people inside. Authorities later discovered the bodies of more victims at the group's other properties in Uganda and concluded that the leaders had orchestrated the killing in response to turmoil caused by their repeated failure to predict the apocalypse.

Source: Cosmopolitan.com

So, what are the traits or characteristics of a cult?
1. The leader(s) teach more about honor, loyalty, and the price of betrayal than he or she teaches about YAHWEH.

2. The leader(s) use fear tactics to keep people from leaving; for example, they may say things like, "If you leave this church, you will lose the anointing" or "I just got word that Mrs. Jane Doe had an accident. When she was a member of this church, she was protected, but now that she has left, the devil can do whatever he wants with her."
3. Members are encouraged (or commanded) to stay away from former members.
4. While we should go after the broken, the abused and the lost souls, many cults specifically target these types of people because broken people typically lack knowledge, but they crave acceptance. In other words, they will hang on to the leader's every word, and will be loyal to the organization, not the Bible.
5. Cult leaders often start causing their followers to question the validity of the Bible one scripture at a time. They do this so that they can interpret the Bible in a way that would allow them to control their congregants.
6. Cults leaders often teach or insinuate that they are the only ones who can rightly divide the Bible.
7. Cult leaders oftentimes encourage or turn a blind eye to sexual immorality and may even engage in it themselves.
8. Cult leaders often encourage their followers to separate themselves from anyone who does not join the cult or agree with their practices. Eventually, they manipulate their followers into disconnecting from everyone, including their families.
9. In cults, new members are often hazed until they have finally proven their loyalty to the leaders and the organization.
10. Women are often seen as nothing but tools for breeding, cooking, and cleaning. Women are often silenced and encouraged to silence any other woman who would dare question their doctrine,
11. False prophecies are oftentimes given by the leadership, and when those prophecies do not come to pass, the leaders refuse to apologize, repent, or recant their statements.
12. There is an over-emphasis placed on the supernatural, and very little emphasis is placed on the scriptures.
13. Public shame is a weapon used to bring people back under submission.
14. Marriages and relationships are destroyed by the leadership.
15. In some extreme cases, members are encouraged to wear uniforms or dress, talk and reason like their leaders.
16. There is a great emphasis placed on the apocalypse, and the book of Revelation is used to scare and control members.
17. Members are taught that they are the only true religion, and every other religion is going to hell or doomed.
18. The scriptures are often misinterpreted. Cults are oftentimes legalistic and stiff-necked.
19. Cult leaders use the fear of being ex-communicated or disfellowshipped to control and

manipulate their followers.

20. Cult leaders are often worshiped and placed on a pedestal above Jesus. In some extreme instances, cult leaders may even claim to be Jesus.
21. Cult leaders are oftentimes paranoid, and they deal heavily with suspicion. This is because inwardly, they know what they are doing is wrong, so they fear being "found out." Because of this, they are always questioning or suspecting their members of gossiping about them, sharing intimate information, or plotting to leave the assembly.
22. Cult members are oftentimes overly zealous and would not dare to question their leadership out of fear of being ex-communicated or worse. Cult members are also more loyal to their leaders than they are to Christ.
23. Members are told how to dress.
24. The leader is not accountable to anyone.
25. In some extreme cases, members are required to live near each other or in a compound.
26. Every measure of the members' lives is controlled by the organization.
27. Members are required to devote their lives or excessive amounts of time to the organization.
28. Marriages are arranged by leadership, and members are encouraged (or required) to not marry anyone who is not a part of the organization.
29. Women are used to seduce non-members and bring them into the organization.
30. Leaders encourage members to use scare tactics to intimidate former members and anyone who considers leaving the organization.
31. Members are not necessarily encouraged to give up ungodly ways; instead, they are positioned in the organization in accordance with their strongholds. For example, a leader may surround himself with former convicts or men and women who are prone to violence. Rather than helping them to heal, the leader will publicly brandish and boast about his "goons" in an attempt to intimidate both insiders and outsiders.
32. Children are sometimes groomed for or by sexual predators.
33. The leaders use gossip, slander, and accusation to divide members from other members.
34. Members must ask for permission before engaging in certain activities like visiting other churches (which is oftentimes forbidden or heavily discouraged). It is wise to be accountable to your leaders, especially if you are on the leadership team, but you should never feel obligated to share every aspect of your life with another human being.
35. Divination, sorcery, astrology, necromancy and/or other ungodly practices are encouraged and justified.
36. Certain scriptures are given a lot of attention, while the rest of the Bible (especially any scriptures that would challenge their interpretation of the scriptures) are never read or

they are rushed through.
37. Critical thinking is strongly opposed and oftentimes punished.
38. Racial supremacy and racial inferiority are taught.
39. Congregants are led to believe that God is going to condemn one race while favoring their own.
40. Followers are brainwashed and led to believe that the dismantling of their original beliefs (purging) is necessary for their redemption.
41. Members are exploited financially, even to the point where they are forced to ignore the needs of their families in order to support the ministry, organization, or leadership.
42. Members are taught to fear the outside world, often being led to believe that everyone outside the ministry or organization is demonized.
43. Followers are led to believe the government is against their organization and therefore cannot be trusted. In some extreme cases, adherents are trained to war against governmental officials and policies.
44. Followers are coerced into trusting leadership with their most intimate secrets, only to have that information weaponized against them.
45. Mind-altering practices are used like mindfulness meditation to help members get through being homesick and to overcome doubt as it relates to the religion or leadership. Keep in mind, as believers, we should meditate on the Word of God, but in false religions, sects, and cults, adherents are encouraged to meditate on everything else but God's Word.
46. Fasting is forced instead of encouraged and is often used to manipulate and control followers.
47. The information followers receive is controlled by the leadership, for example, members are told what they can watch on television, or they may be prohibited from watching television or utilizing the internet. Magazines and pamphlets are created by the leadership in order to control what information members are taking in.
48. Non-biblical titles are used and given out as a reward; this promotes a sense of religious and individual supremacy.
49. People are given religious titles and seats of authority almost immediately upon visiting or joining the organization.
50. Members are encouraged to brand themselves (tattoos, cutting, etc.), and anyone who challenges this belief (or any of their beliefs) is labeled as a charlatan and an enemy.

Cult Facts

According to Steve Eichel, a recognized international cult expert, Psychologist, and President

of the International Cultic Studies Association, there are over 10,000 cults in the United States of America as of 2018.
Not all cults are religious; some are pagan, and some are occultic.
Religious cults are usually spin-offs of one or more denominations.
Within Judaism, there were three main sects of Jews around the time that Jesus walked the Earth; they were: the Pharisees, Sadducees, and the Essenes. In many respects, these were all cults.
Women are more likely to join a cult than men.
Cults serve as false safe havens for people who deal majorly with rejection.
Most cult members do not realize they're in cults.

Deliverance from Cults

You may be in a cult, or maybe you know someone who is in a cult, and you want to usher in freedom for yourself or your loved one. Can you be delivered from cults? Absolutely! But deliverance from a cult is not a simple resignation letter and a change of address, after all, you can physically detach yourself from a cult but still be mentally bound by its policies, beliefs, and the traumas you suffered while in that cult. This means deliverance is two-part. You must be delivered both physically and mentally. But, how do you do that? Below are ten steps to freedom.

1. First and foremost, you must determine whether leaving puts your life or the lives of your loved ones at risk. If it does, you will need to enlist the aid of your local police department.
2. Before you do anything or say anything, pray! Never omit or disregard the counsel of the Holy Spirit!
3. There is no "formal" protocol when leaving a cult. However, if you are leaving a church because you do not fully agree with its teachings, it does not necessarily mean the church is a cult. In this case, send a resignation letter, either via email or mail; that is if it is safe to do so.
4. Never announce that you are leaving a cult! This could severely put you at risk! Just leave and do not look back!
5. Return any items that you have received from the cult! Do not keep anything!
6. Remove the cult members from your social media pages or shut down your social media accounts until further notice! When and if you reopen those accounts, be sure to

purge your page of every cult member.
7. Document any odd occurrences, like cult members passing by your home. This behavior is rare, but in some extreme cases, it can and does happen!
8. Get counseling! Trauma does not heal itself!
9. Renounce any, and every ungodly oath you have made with and/or for the organization.
10. You will need deliverance! Make sure you find a credible deliverance ministry in your area so you can be set free from every spirit that entered in through your association with that cult.
11. Pray and find a good church home. You need a community of people backing you! Cults use their numbers to intimidate people. Surround yourself with Godly people, remembering one can put one thousand to flight, but two can put ten thousand to flight.
12. Heal. Do not rush the process, but don't delay the process either!

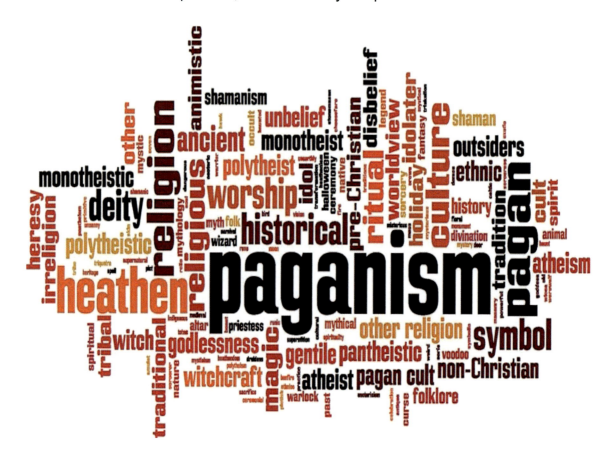

UNDERSTANDING THE OCCULT AND PAGAN PRACTICES

Culture	Cult	Occult	Cultivate

I listed the chart above to show you the relationship between culture and demonic practices. Many times, cults were established in small groups before they became widespread and before many of their practices were adopted as cultures. The same is true for many of the occult practices we find prevailing all around the world today. They are usually derived from an individual who has a thought, an imagination, or an idea he does not cast down. That thought, because it is not addressed, begins to root itself in the person's mind until it completely infects the individual's belief system. Amazingly enough, as humans, we are obsessed with sharing; it is an instinctual practice that we engage in, so whatever it is we experience (whether good or bad), if we feel it has, will, or can benefit others in any way, we will often share it with those closest to us. Over time, we will start sharing that information with random strangers. This is exactly what Eve did in the Garden of Eden. After she was deceived by Satan, she felt this insatiable and almost instinctual need to share what she had just been taught with her husband. She did not just share her new doctrinal beliefs with him, she also shared the very thing the couple was commanded not to touch—the forbidden fruit. The moment their belief systems became infected or corrupted was the moment they became accursed. This is because their new beliefs would only set the stage for other lies, and they would eventually develop many practices and habits as a result. of those beliefs. Those practices would become what we now refer to as "cultures." Once they had children, over time, those cultures would give birth to traditions; this would also set the stage for their family to break off into sects because many of their children and grandchildren would grow up and begin to question, challenge, and disprove their beliefs. These sects are called cults. This is how familial cults are started, and it goes without saying that familial cults eventually grow to reach others outside the familial unit.

The Genesis of Occult Practices

Genesis 2:4-5

These are the generations of the heavens and of the earth when they were created, in the day that the LORD God made the earth and the heavens, and every plant of the field before it was in the earth, and every herb of the field before it grew: for the LORD God had not caused it to rain upon the earth, and there was not a man to till the ground.

Another word often used synonymous with "gene" is "hereditary."

| Heredity | Heritage | Inheritance | Hereditary |

Notice the scripture referred to every plant and every herb of the field as "generations of the heavens," meaning that God literally took seeds He created and planted in Heaven and placed those seeds in the Earth. But, before those plants could grow, the Earth needed rain (water). All the same, the ground needed tilling. Another word for "till" is "cultivate." Ground or dirt, in the scriptures, is often used to symbolize flesh, so when God told Adam to dress and keep the Garden, He was also telling Adam to dress or address his flesh. But wait! Sin was not on the Earth yet, so why would Adam need to have any measure of self-control? It's simple—because Adam had been granted a supernatural ability called "will," and obviously Satan was already present in the Earth. God knew that Adam and Eve would eventually cross paths with His adversary and the couple would be given the opportunity to make a decision contrary to the command He gave them. After all, what is the purpose of having will if you do not have anywhere to exercise that will or anything to choose from? And before long, Satan (being a spirit) entered into the body of a snake and made his way to the Garden. There, he found Eve walking around naked, unashamed, and content. He wanted her in the worse way, but not sexually! Just as he entered the body of the snake, he wanted to enter into her body, but he couldn't because she had not submitted her will to him. In order to enter her, he needed to get her to willfully accept a lie. This would bring her into sin, and because he is the author of lies, this would bring her into agreement with him, thus, allowing him to enter the body of a human. But, why was he interested in Adam and Eve's bodies? Because they were made in the image of God. Therefore, their bodies closely resembled the body he'd forfeited when he chose to become Satan (God's adversary) rather than just continuing to serve as Lucifer (God's light-bearer, morning star). He saw God's glory all around Eve! This is why she did not realize she was naked because she was wrapped in the glory of God! Lusting after her position, Satan made his way over to Eve. We all know the story. Satan was successfully able to deceive Eve, causing her to rebel against God's command, and once she had sinned, she could not resist sharing her transgression with her husband. Adam (which means ground) bit into the lie, and from there, the garden of their flesh became pregnant with iniquity. What iniquities were in them? The Bible refers to them as the works of the flesh. Again, they are:

Adultery	Fornication	Uncleanness
Lasciviousness	Idolatry	Witchcraft
Hatred	Variance	Emulations
Wrath	Strife	Sedition

Heresies	Envyings	Murders
Drunkenness		Revelings

These weren't just works, they would eventually become customs, cultures and traditions that would automatically pass down from one generation to the next. Consider this—the word "generation" comes from the word "gene." Let us take a closer look at that word!

Gene	Genesis	Genetics	Generation

Gene
(in informal use) a unit of heredity which is transferred from a parent to offspring and is held to determine some characteristic of the offspring.
Source: Oxford Languages

Gene
*genə-, also *gen-, Proto-Indo-European root meaning "give birth, beget," with derivatives referring to procreation and familial and tribal groups.
Source: Online Etymology Dictionary

Now that sin had gotten into the ground (Adam), he would need to cultivate his flesh. This is because Satan had managed to plant every evil seed in the couple, and those seeds would continually produce fruit. Again, these fruits are called the works of the flesh. One of these fruits, as you will notice from the list above, is witchcraft.

Witchcraft	Occult
the practice of magic, especially black magic; the use of spells. (in a modern context) religious practice involving magic and affinity with nature, usually within a pagan tradition.	Of, relating to, or dealing with supernatural influences, agencies, or phenomena. • Beyond the realm of human comprehension; inscrutable. • Available only to the initiate; secret: occult lore. • Hidden from view; concealed.
Source: Oxford Languages	Source: Definition.org

This means the genesis of the occult is Satan!

The Origin of Witchcraft

First, what is culture? According to Live Science, culture is "the characteristics and knowledge of a particular group of people, encompassing language, religion, cuisine, social habits, music, and arts." Tradition, on the other hand, is defined by Oxford Languages as "the transmission of customs or beliefs from generation to generation, or the fact of being passed on in this way." What I want you to gather from this is that both cults and occults are often man-made, demonically influenced establishments that originate from a shared belief between two or more people. This is their genesis or beginning. But, because their beliefs are not necessarily widely accepted, the group will often set out to indoctrinate others by first creating a soul tie with those people. They will oftentimes use sex, trauma, or religion to establish these bonds. And when these bonds are created, the next step of a false teacher is to establish cultures; these are the practices that distinguish one faith, belief system, or religion from another. If these practices are passed down, they become traditions.

Isaiah 14:12-18	Revelation 12:7-12	Genesis 2:8-17
How art thou fallen from heaven, O Lucifer, son of the morning! How art thou cut down to the ground, which didst weaken the nations! For thou hast said in thine heart, I will ascend into heaven, I will exalt my throne above the stars of God: I will sit also upon the mount of the congregation, in the sides of the north: I will ascend above the heights of the clouds; I will be like the most High. Yet thou shalt be brought down to hell, to the sides of the pit. They that see thee shall narrowly look upon thee, and consider thee, saying, Is this the man that made the earth to tremble, that did shake kingdoms; that made the	And there was war in heaven: Michael and his angels fought against the dragon; and the dragon fought and his angels, And prevailed not; neither was their place found any more in heaven. And the great dragon was cast out, that old serpent, called the Devil, and Satan, which deceiveth the whole world: he was cast out into the earth, and his angels were cast out with him. And I heard a loud voice saying in heaven, Now is come salvation, and strength, and the kingdom of our God, and the power of his Christ: for the accuser of our brethren is cast down, which accused them before our God day and night. And they overcame him by the blood of	And the LORD God planted a garden eastward in Eden; and there he put the man whom he had formed. And out of the ground made the LORD God to grow every tree that is pleasant to the sight, and good for food; the tree of life also in the midst of the garden, and the tree of knowledge of good and evil. And a river went out of Eden to water the garden; and from thence it was parted, and became into four heads. The name of the first is Pison: that is it which compasseth the whole land of Havilah, where there is gold; And the gold of that land is good: there is bdellium and the onyx stone. And the name of the second

world as a wilderness, and destroyed the cities thereof; that opened not the house of his prisoners? All the kings of the nations, even all of them, lie in glory, every one in his own house.	the Lamb, and by the word of their testimony; and they loved not their lives unto the death. Therefore rejoice, *ye* heavens, and ye that dwell in them. Woe to the inhabiters of the earth and of the sea! for the devil is come down unto you, having great wrath, because he knoweth that he hath but a short time.	river is Gihon: the same is it that compasseth the whole land of Ethiopia. And the name of the third river is Hiddekel: that is it which goeth toward the east of Assyria. And the fourth river is Euphrates. And the LORD God took the man, and put him into the garden of Eden to dress it and to keep it. And the LORD God commanded the man, saying, Of every tree of the garden thou mayest freely eat: But of the tree of the knowledge of good and evil, thou shalt not eat of it: for in the day that thou eatest thereof thou shalt surely die.

In the scriptures above, we see a pattern. First, Lucifer has an evil thought. Of course, he was an angel of the Lord, specifically designed to lead and be an instrument of worship. His body was literally made of jewels and instruments. Don't believe me? Read the scripture below.

Ezekiel 28:13-14
Thou hast been in Eden the garden of God; every precious stone was thy covering, the sardius, topaz, and the diamond, the beryl, the onyx, and the jasper, the sapphire, the emerald, and the carbuncle, and gold: the workmanship of thy tabrets and of thy pipes was prepared in thee in the day that thou wast created. Thou art the anointed cherub that covereth; and I have set thee so: thou wast upon the holy mountain of God; thou hast walked up and down in the midst of the stones of fire.

In this scripture, we find God addressing Lucifer. Notice his body was covered with every precious stone that could be found on the Earth, and his body was made of tabrets (similar, to tambourines) and pipes. God is Spirit. The Greek word for "spirit" is "pneuma" and it literally means "breath" or "wind." So, consider this—God would literally pass through Lucifer's body;

his body was a literal instrument of God. The sound of God passing through Lucifer's body would create pure worship. Also, the Bible tells us that God is Light, so whenever God passed through Lucifer's body, His glory would be reflected through him. The angels of God would then bow down before Lucifer, but they were not worshiping him, they were worshiping God. Nevertheless, Lucifer began to covet this praise. He became lifted up in his heart, and he decided to create a new doctrine; this doctrine is what the Bible refers to as the "doctrine of demons." This doctrine is filled with lies and twisted truths. He used these lies to lead one-third of God's angels astray. He then spread his doctrine and his influence when he made his way into the Garden of Eden. What he was doing was creating a contrary wind. This contrary wind is called witchcraft. This was why 1 Samuel 15:23 says, "For rebellion is as the sin of witchcraft." It is a power, a force or a wind that goes against God. No angel of God moves against Him; the only angels that move contrary to His will are called devils!

The Revelation of Occult Practices

Satan was an external wind or force that was cast out of Heaven into the Earth. Adam and Eve walked with God, meaning, they agreed with Him.

Genesis 2:7
And the LORD God formed man of the dust of the ground, and breathed into his nostrils the breath of life; and man became a living soul.

Amos 3:3
Can two walk together, except they be agreed?

When God breathed into Adam, the two of them began to walk together; they were as one, meaning, they were in agreement. But, when Adam sinned, he went in the opposite direction. Seeing that Adam was no longer walking with Him, God went looking for his son.

Genesis 3:8-9
And they heard the voice of the LORD God walking in the garden in the cool of the day: and Adam and his wife hid themselves from the presence of the LORD God amongst the trees of the garden. And the LORD God called unto Adam, and said unto him, Where art thou?

Where art thou or, better yet, where are you? When God asked this question, He was not trying to physically locate Adam, since man was led by his spirit. He was trying to locate Adam spiritually. We already established that there is a difference between man and mankind.

Man		
Body	Soul	Spirit
Third	Second	First (Leader)

→ **(Righteousness)**

Mankind		
Body	Soul	Spirit
First (Leader)	Second	Third

(Perversion)← ←

As you can see, man was moving in God's will, but when he sinned, everything shifted! He began to move opposite of how God designed him. This is called perversion! In this, we find mankind is led by his flesh, whereas man was led by his spirit. Another word for mankind is human, which means humbled or humiliated man. Therefore, when God uttered those famous words, "Adam, where are you?" He was acknowledging that Adam was no longer on the right path; Adam was no longer walking with Him. But, Adam was now led by his flesh; this was why he told God where he was physically hiding. He no longer understood the things of God because "the natural man receiveth not the things of the Spirit of God: for they are foolishness unto him" (see 1 Corinthians 2:14). Again, Adam's response revealed just where he was—he was in the flesh and no longer led by his spirit!

Genesis 3:10

And he said, I heard thy voice in the garden, and I was afraid, because I was naked; and I hid myself.

Adam now identified with his flesh, meaning, he could no longer identify with God. And now, all that was evil that had been planted in his flesh would begin to bear fruit. To counter this, God, in His arraignment of Adam and Eve, told the couple that they would now have to cultivate their flesh through hard work; this was a prophetic reference to the law of Moses.

Genesis 3:17-19

And unto Adam he said, Because thou hast hearkened unto the voice of thy wife, and hast eaten of the tree, of which I commanded thee, saying, Thou shalt not eat of it: cursed is the ground for thy sake; in sorrow shalt thou eat of it all the days of thy life; thorns also and thistles shall it bring forth to thee; and thou shalt eat the herb of the field; in the sweat of thy face shalt thou eat bread, till thou return unto the ground; for out of it wast thou taken: for dust

> thou art, and unto dust shalt thou return.

Adam and Eve went on to produce their first two sons; they were Cain and Abel.

> ### Genesis 4:1-8
>
> And Adam knew Eve his wife; and she conceived, and bare Cain, and said, I have gotten a man from the LORD. And she again bare his brother Abel. And Abel was a keeper of sheep, but Cain was a tiller of the ground. And in process of time it came to pass, that Cain brought of the fruit of the ground an offering unto the LORD. And Abel, he also brought of the firstlings of his flock and of the fat thereof. And the LORD had respect unto Abel and to his offering: But unto Cain and to his offering he had not respect. And Cain was very wroth, and his countenance fell. And the LORD said unto Cain, Why art thou wroth? and why is thy countenance fallen? If thou doest well, shalt thou not be accepted? And if thou doest not well, sin lieth at the door. And unto thee shall be his desire, and thou shalt rule over him.
> And Cain talked with Abel his brother: and it came to pass, when they were in the field, that Cain rose up against Abel his brother, and slew him.

Cain and Abel were a picture of what was now in the couple. Abel represented worship and all that was of God, but Cain represented the works of the flesh. The evil in Adam rose to defeat the good that was in him. Abel lifted pure worship to God. By giving God a living sacrifice, he was essentially repenting before the Lord. This was a picture of him offering his flesh up to the Lord as a sacrifice. But Cain, on the other hand, decided to give God an offering that had come out of the very ground that God had cursed. He essentially tried to impress God with his flesh or, better yet, his works. In other words, he did not sacrifice his flesh (his natural desires); instead, he decided to offer God perverted fruits. God rejected Cain's offering, and because of this, Cain decided to murder his brother, Abel. Side note: isn't this exactly what people do with sage? They use sage in their attempts to tamper with the spirit realm, instead of just yielding to the Holy Spirit in prayer and obedience. This is how occultic practices begin! They start with people who want to access the blessings of God without having to submit to the will of God.

Rebellion is As the Sin of Witchcraft
Genesis 11:4-9

> And the whole earth was of one language, and of one speech. And it came to pass, as they journeyed from the east, that they found a plain in the land of Shinar; and they dwelt there. And they said one to another, Go to, let us make brick, and burn them thoroughly. And they had brick for stone, and slime had they for mortar. And they said, Go to, let us build us a city and a tower, whose top may reach unto heaven; and let us make us a name, lest we be scattered abroad upon the face of the whole earth. And the LORD came down to see the city and the tower, which the children of men builded. And the LORD said, Behold, the people is one, and they have all one language; and this they begin to do: and now nothing will be restrained from them, which they have imagined to do. Go to, let us go down, and there confound their language, that they may not understand one another's speech. So the LORD scattered them abroad from thence upon the face of all the earth: and they left off to build the city. Therefore is the name of it called Babel; because the LORD did there confound the language of all the earth: and from thence did the LORD scatter them abroad upon the face of all the earth.

Isaiah 14:13-14 is reminiscent of Lucifer's plight. Lucifer had once said in his heart, "I will ascend into heaven, I will exalt my throne above the stars of God: I will sit also upon the mount of the congregation, in the sides of the north: I will ascend above the heights of the clouds; I will be like the Most High." The problem was he already had an assignment, a purpose, and an identity, but there he was rebelling against his design so that he could compete with the Most-High God. And now, well over two-thousand years after the Earth had been created, there stood a group of people who started to dialog amongst themselves, and they decided that they did not need God to get to Heaven. All they needed was their own abilities. It is safe to say that they did not understand the concept of Heaven, since Heaven is not up in direction. After all, Heaven is not a natural place. Remember, "in the beginning," God created the Heavens and the Earth. Who is Elohim? He is Alpha (the Beginning) and Omega (the End)! So, God created the Heavens and the Earth inside of Himself! Nevertheless, the people of the Earth reasoned in the same manner that Lucifer had once reasoned in; they pretty much said, "We will ascend into Heaven; we will exalt ourselves above God. We will be our own gods!" Consequently, the very thing they feared came upon them. This is a picture of rebellion, and this was why it is the same as the sin of witchcraft. Rebellion is the very foundation of the occult.

Genesis 9:20-25

> And Noah began to be an husbandman, and he planted a vineyard: And he drank of the wine, and was drunken; and he was uncovered within his tent. And Ham, the father of Canaan, saw the nakedness of his father, and told his two brethren without. And Shem and Japheth took a garment, and laid it upon both their shoulders, and went backward, and covered the nakedness of their father; and their faces were backward, and they saw not their father's

> nakedness. And Noah awoke from his wine, and knew what his younger son had done unto him. And he said, Cursed be Canaan; a servant of servants shall he be unto his brethren.

Nimrod, the son of Cush and the great-grandson of Noah, is believed to be the man who headed up building the Tower of Babel. There is no real evidence to support this, but theologians, scholars, and historians all agree that Nimrod was present during the building of the Tower. Many agree that he likely spearheaded the project. The Bible does not specifically call him a king, but it does refer to his kingdoms, with Babel being one of them, so it is more probable that he was not only the brains behind the building of the Tower, but he did ultimately establish himself as a king. Ironically enough, the name "Nimrod" comes from a Semitic root, and it literally means "to rebel."

The name "Satan" means adversary, and we see Lucifer being referred to as Satan immediately after he went to war against God's angels in Heaven. The root word of "adversary" is "adverse" and Oxford Languages define it as "preventing success or development; harmful; unfavorable." Lucifer's crime was that he tried to alter the will (and nature) of God. God gave him an assignment, and he was specifically designed for that very assignment. Nevertheless, like us and all of God's angels, he had the technology of "will." Think of it this way—imagine a huge rotating knob sticking out of the Earth. Now imagine God turning that knob to the right. And finally, imagine Satan attempting to push or turn that knob to the left. This is what we refer to as witchcraft. It is an adverse reaction or an opposing force to God's will. So, when Lucifer lied to God's angels, he was engaging in witchcraft. When one-third of God's angels rebelled against Him, they were engaging in witchcraft. And while "witchcraft" may be more of an earthly term, the correct term for this is rebellion; this is why the Bible says that witchcraft is as the sin of rebellion. Hear me—even if you are doing the wrong thing to get what is rightfully yours, you are engaging in witchcraft. And of course, there are different expressions or manifestations of witchcraft, with the most recognized form being sorcery, incantations, astrology, and the like. Nevertheless, these are what we call higher levels of witchcraft; these forms of witchcraft are human attempts to manipulate and control the realm of the spirit. Howbeit, there are other occultic expressions, which include attempting to control and manipulate people, whether this is done through sex, flattery, money, false religion or whatever the case may be. So, when the scriptures talk about the Tower of Babel, we can safely conclude this action was, in and of itself, rebellion or, better yet, witchcraft. Again, witchcraft is not just some old lady chanting gibberish over some potion or concoction she's whipped up; witchcraft is turning the knob to the left when God told us to turn it to the right. Now, because we were born in sin and shaped in iniquity, that knob starts to look a lot like a steering wheel. Whereas, as we navigate through life, every speed bump, air pressure, and foreign object in the road will oftentimes cause us to jerk that wheel to the left just a little to avoid what we see immediately before us. This is called fear.

Nevertheless, over the course of time, we soon learn to grip that wheel a little tighter and keep it on the road without swerving to the left or right. But, when we intentionally, consistently, and progressively go left, we are rebelling against God, meaning, we have entered into agreement with God's adversary. This does not take away our salvation, but it does take us further and further away from God until we finally find ourselves with reprobate minds.

Facts About the Tower of Babel

1. The word "Babel" means "confusion" and "mixture." It is where we get the word "babbling."
2. The Tower of Babel was more than just a tower, it was an entire city.
3. More theologians believe that the Tower of Babel (city) was the corrupt and ungodly city that would later be known as Babylon.
4. Mankind attempted to build the Tower of Babel before the Law of Moses was given.
5. The Tower was an attempt of mankind to enter Heaven through their works.
6. The Tower may have been a trauma response to the Great Flood. Theologians summarize that, in addition to trying to illegally reach Heaven, the builders of the Tower were also trying to ensure that if the Earth were flooded again, they would not perish in its waters.
7. The builders of the Tower of Babel were the descendants of Noah, since the Earth had previously been destroyed with a flood, leaving only Noah and his family alive.
8. The people of the Earth built the Tower of Babel for a total of 107 years before God confused their language.
9. When God confused the language of the people, it did not look like we'd imagined. He did not see two men working alongside one another and confuse their language so they could no longer work together. Instead, He gave different languages to the descendants of Noah's children. Remember, Noah cursed the descendants of Ham, therefore, they likely had their own language or languages, just as the descendants of Shem had their own language or languages; the same was true for the descendants of Japheth. They moved into different regions of the Earth, and this is how the different races began to take shape.
10. The Tower of Babel serves as a towering symbol of pride. It represented human accomplishment, rebellion and mankind's attempt to, once again, be like God.

The Way, the Truth, and the Life

John 1:1-5

In the beginning was the Word, and the Word was with God, and the Word was God. The

> same was in the beginning with God. All things were made by him; and without him was not anything made that was made. In him was life; and the life was the light of men. And the light shineth in darkness; and the darkness comprehended it not.

Before attempting to build a city that reached up to Heaven, the people thought to themselves, "There has to be another way!" In this, they were referring to entering Heaven, but not necessarily entering into an agreement or covenant with God. Their hearts echoed the sentiments of many believers and non-believers today. Living a life that was pleasing to God almost seemed impossible. They considered the men and the women who perished in the Great Flood, and even though God promised to never destroy the Earth with a flood again, they knew there were other ways He could completely wipe them off the face of the planet. Frustrated, anxious, tired, and perverted, they tried to create their own way. In short, the Tower of Babel became the very first idol to be erected after the flood, and while the men and women of that time did not get on their faces and bow before it, they completely trusted it to deliver them. In short, they formed their very first cult and occult. They were a cult because they did not fully follow God; instead, they were religious and rebellious. What they practiced was occultism because they used their knowledge and the strength that God had given them to move against His will. Did they practice divination? The Bible does not expressly say this, but what we do know is the building materials they used were commonly used to build ziqqurats.

Ziqqurat

A ziggurat is a very ancient and massive building structure of a particular shape that served as part of a temple complex in the various local religions of Mesopotamia and the flat highlands of what is now western Iran. Sumer, Babylonia, and Assyria are known to have about 25 ziggurats, evenly divided among them.

The shape of a ziggurat makes it clearly identifiable: a roughly square platform base with sides that recede inward as the structure rises, and a flat top presumed to have supported some form of a shrine. Sun-baked bricks form the core of a ziggurat, with fire-baked bricks forming the outer faces. Unlike the Egyptian pyramids, a ziggurat was a solid structure with no internal chambers. An external staircase or spiral ramp provided access to the top platform. The word ziggurat is from an extinct Semitic language, and derives from a verb that means "to build on a flat space."

The handful of ziggurats still visible are all in various states of ruin, but based on the dimensions of their bases, it is believed that they may have been as much as 150 ft. high. It is likely that the terraced sides were planted with shrubs and flowering plants, and many scholars believe that the legendary Hanging Gardens of Babylon was a ziggurat structure.

History and Function

Ziggurats are some of the oldest of ancient religious structures in the world, with the first

> examples dating to about 2200 BCE and the last constructions dating to approximately 500 BCE. Only a few of the Egyptian pyramids predate the oldest ziggurats.
>
> Ziggurats were constructed by many local regions of the Mesopotamia regions. The exact purpose of a ziggurat is unknown since these religions did not document their belief systems in the same manner as, for example, the Egyptians did. It is a fair assumption, though, to think that ziggurats, like most temple structures for various religions, was conceived of as homes for the local gods. There is no evidence to suggest they were used as locations for public worship or ritual, and it is believed that only priests were generally in attendance at a ziggurat. Except for small chambers around the bottom outer level, these were solid structures with no large internal spaces.
>
> Source: Thought.co

What this means is that the Tower of Babel may have been more than man's attempt to illegally enter Heaven. It may have been another one of man's unrelenting attempts to mix what is holy with what is profane. It may have been their attempt to build a temple for the many gods they presumably worshiped that stretched all the way up to Heaven, but this is just an assumption. Regardless of what their overall goal was, what we can all agree on is that it was displeasing to God, so He confused their language. In this, He separated the tares from the wheat.

Today, there are still billions of men and women who are looking for "another way" to enter Heaven. Many false religions preach about their own version of heaven—one that allows them to indulge in their fleshly desires and cater to their hearts' most wicked desires. All the same, there are millions upon millions of people trying to figure out which way is the right way to Heaven. The problem with this is, they want the benefits of the Kingdom without having to pursue the heart of the King. Consequently, they are led astray by their own desires. And because we are spiritual creatures, many people turn to spirituality in an attempt to answer some of the many questions that plague their hearts, but spirituality outside of God (who is Light) is dark. The dark side of the spirit realm is what the Bible refers to as the kingdom of darkness. This is Satan's abode—the abode of demons. Now, it is not a physical place where demons dwell; the kingdom of darkness is a system that moves contrary to the will of God. And hear me—because there is no light in that system, Satan and his accomplices tend to disguise themselves as angels of light to draw men and women into false religions and into black magic/dark arts. And not only do people look for another way to Heaven, but they also look for another way to solve many of life's most complex mysteries and problems. They turn to sex, drugs, alcohol, food, and pretty much anything that will give them an adrenaline boost in their attempts to either rid themselves of their problems or to numb the emotions that emerge as a result of those problems. All the same, adrenaline and oxytocin tend to give people a false high; this is what many people use as a substitute for the Holy Spirit. Nevertheless, there is only one Way to the Father, and that is through His Son, Jesus Christ. Any other "way" that presents itself is nothing but an illegal point of entry that will only allow those who enter in through it to access the spirit realm without the guidance and protection of the Holy Spirit. This is why our mental institutions are overflowing with people today. People keep going in through the dark side of the spirit realm, running into angels disguising themselves as angels of lights (demons) and being led into occultic practices like Wicca, third-eye meditations, and sage burning. And while many of these practices do offer some temporary relief, the long-term effects of practicing witchcraft are often seen spread out from generation to generation, and they usually manifest themselves as in the family as:

Mental Illness	Sexual Perversion (Rape, Molestation, Incest, etc.)
Premature Death	Divorce
Murder	Destruction of the Family Unit
Suicide	Poverty

Anyone who has ever operated in the ministry of deliverance can attest to the fact that when you see these issues prevailing in a family, chances are, one of the matriarchs or patriarchs in that family practiced witchcraft! What they did not realize is that in order to access the knowledge shared in the kingdom of darkness, you must first enter into an agreement with that kingdom. Hear me—both the kingdom of darkness and the Kingdom of God has fruits; these are their wages! This is what you earn or inherit through your servitude! In the kingdom of darkness, the fruit is DEATH! Romans 6:23 confirms this; it reads, "For the wages of sin is death; but the gift of God is eternal life through Jesus Christ our Lord." Satan can offer you the world, but everything he gives you has something evil attached to it. This was why it is called bait! This is also why God went on record, saying "The blessing of the LORD makes rich, and he adds no sorrow with it" (Proverbs 10:22). In other words, anything that you get outside of God has sorrow, misery, depression, frustration, fear, and every evil fruit of Satan's kingdom attached to it! In short, there is only one Way to God, one Way to the blessings of God, and one Way to everlasting life, and His name is the name above all names—Jesus Christ! If you go any other way, you will enter into an agreement with the enemy of your soul, and while he may offer you some relief, the aftertaste will be bitter!

John 14:6
Jesus saith unto him, I am the way, the truth, and the life: no man cometh unto the Father, but by me.

List of Common Pagan Practices

Smudging	Burning Sage	Astrology
Chakra Healing	Ancestral Worship	Yoga (Religious)
Fortune-Telling	Necromancy	Numerology

12 Reasons People Turn to the Occult (Witchcraft)

Fear	Impatience	Lack of Knowledge
Covetousness (Envy)	Unforgiveness (Wrath)	Lust for Power
Lust for Fame	Love of Money	Frustration
Grief	Bad Association	To Rebel Against God

Scriptures About Witchcraft

Leviticus 19:31

Regard not them that have familiar spirits, neither seek after wizards, to be defiled by them: I [am] the LORD your God.

Leviticus 20:6

And the soul that turneth after such as have familiar spirits, and after wizards, to go a whoring after them, I will even set my face against that soul, and will cut him off from among his people.

Leviticus 20:27

A man also or woman that hath a familiar spirit, or that is a wizard, shall surely be put to death: they shall stone them with stones: their blood shall be upon them.

Deuteronomy 18:9-12

When thou art come into the land which the LORD thy God giveth thee, thou shalt not learn to do after the abominations of those nations. There shall not be found among you [any one] that maketh his son or his daughter to pass through the fire, [or] that useth divination, [or] an observer of times, or an enchanter, or a witch, or a charmer, or a consulter with familiar spirits, or a wizard, or a necromancer. For all that do these things [are] an abomination unto the LORD: and because of these abominations the LORD thy God doth drive them out from before thee.

Isaiah 8:19

"And when they shall say unto you, Seek unto them that have familiar spirits, and unto wizards that peep, and that mutter: should not a people seek unto their God? for the living to the dead?"

Revelation 18:23
And the light of a candle shall shine no more at all in thee; and the voice of the bridegroom and of the bride shall be heard no more at all in thee: for thy merchants were the great men of the earth; for by thy sorceries were all nations deceived.

Revelation 21:8
But the fearful, and unbelieving, and the abominable, and murderers, and whoremongers, and sorcerers, and idolaters, and all liars, shall have their part in the lake which burneth with fire and brimstone: which is the second death.

Challenge Yourself

Using the calendar below, list every significant event that has taken place for you this week, and list every significant event that takes place over the next four weeks.

Sunday	Monday	Tuesday	Wednesday	Thursday	Friday	Saturday

12 Tribes of Israel

Reuben	Simeon	Judah
Issachar	Zebulun	Benjamin
Dan	Naphtali	Gad
Asher	Ephraim	Manasseh

The Gifts of God

Five-Fold Ministerial Gifts

Apostle	Prophet	Pastor	Evangelist	Teacher

Ephesians 4:11-15

And he gave some, apostles; and some, prophets; and some, evangelists; and some, pastors and teachers; tor the perfecting of the saints, for the work of the ministry, for the edifying of the body of Christ: Till we all come in the unity of the faith, and of the knowledge of the Son of God, unto a perfect man, unto the measure of the stature of the fulness of Christ: That we henceforth be no more children, tossed to and fro, and carried about with every wind of doctrine, by the sleight of men, and cunning craftiness, whereby they lie in wait to deceive; But speaking the truth in love, may grow up into him in all things, which is the head, even Christ.

Gifts of the Spirit

Word of Wisdom	Word of Knowledge	Faith
Gifts of Healing	Working of Miracles	Prophecy
Discerning of Spirits	Divers Kinds of Tongues	Interpretation of Tongues

1 Corinthians 12:4-11

Now there are diversities of gifts, but the same Spirit. And there are differences of administrations, but the same Lord. And there are diversities of operations, but it is the same God which worketh all in all. But the manifestation of the Spirit is given to every man to profit withal. For to one is given by the Spirit the word of wisdom; to another the word of knowledge by the same Spirit; to another faith by the same Spirit; to another the gifts of healing by the same Spirit; to another the working of miracles; to another prophecy; to another; to another divers kinds of tongues; to another the interpretation of tongues: But all these worketh that one and the selfsame Spirit, dividing to every man severally as he will.

Full List of 16 Spiritual Gifts			
Administration	Apostleship	Discernment	Exhortation
Evangelism	Faith	Giving	Hospitality
Knowledge	Leadership	Mercy	Prophecy
Serving	Tongues	Teaching	Wisdom

Other Gifts from God

Life (Genesis 2:7)

And the LORD God formed man of the dust of the ground, and breathed into his nostrils the breath of life; and man became a living soul.

Eternal Life (Romans 6:23)

For the wages of sin is death, but the free gift of God is eternal life in Christ Jesus our Lord.

Grace (Ephesians 4:7)

But unto every one of us is given grace according to the measure of the gift of Christ.

Children (Psalm 127:3)

Behold, children are a gift of the Lord, The fruit of the womb is a reward.

God gave us the gift of His love.
God gave us the gift of His Son, Jesus Christ.
Jesus gave us the gift of the Holy Spirit.

God	Jesus	Holy Spirit

BIBLE FACTS

There are 66 books in the Bible	There are 17 historical books in the Bible	Eden means "delight" in Hebrew	The longest book is Psalms
The word "God" appears 4,473 times	The Bible mentions 34 "false gods"	There are 1,260 promises in the Bible	The shortest book in the Bible is 3 John
The word "Lord" appears 7,836 times	China leads the world in Bible production	The Bible has 21 epistles	The word "Genesis" means "origin"
The word "hate" is used 87 times	The word "love" is used 310 times	"Wait on God" is mentioned 40 times	Longest chapter in the Bible is Psalm 119
Timothy's father was a Gentile	Moses wrote the first 5 books of the Bible	Shortest chapter in the Bible is Psalm 117	21 dreams were recorded in the Bible
Salt is mentioned in the Bible 34 times	Isaac was 37 years old when Sarah died	David was 70 years old when he died	Deborah was the only female judge of Israel
The Bible has over 6,000 prophecies	"Amen" is the last word in the Bible	Malachi contains the most prophecies	Angels are mentioned in 34 Bible books
Most of the Old Testament is written in Hebrew	The original Books of the Bible didn't have chapters or verses	There are more than 3,200 fulfilled prophecies	It took around 50-75 years to complete the New Testament
The Bible has been translated into 704 languages	It took over 1,000 years to finish the Old Testament	"Fear not" is mentioned 365 times in the Bible	The word "faith" is mentioned 336 times in the KJV

More Bible Facts

1. Jesus "marveled" at only two things; they were the faith of a centurion and the unbelief of the people in Nazareth.
2. The Bible was written on three continents: Asia, Africa, and Europe.
3. The Bible never said that Jonah was swallowed by a whale; it says that he was swallowed by a "great fish."
4. The Bible consists of more than 8,000 predictions.
5. Before the "great fall," Adam did not have to pray to God since he walked with Him.
6. The word "testament" means "covenant" or "contract."
7. The Bible is the only religious text that mentions the origin of the world and the creation of man.
8. The word "Israel" means "strives with God."
9. The first person to ever be referred to as a Hebrew was Abram.
10. God told Isaiah to walk around naked for three years.
11. Isaiah 40:22 tells us that the Earth is round.
12. Enoch was the first man in the Bible to prophesy.
13. The word Bible comes from the Greek word Ta Biblia, which means "books".
14. Apostle Paul was the last man to perform miracles in the Bible.
15. The Bible never said that Adam and Eve ate an apple from the Tree of the Knowledge of Good and Evil, only they ate a fruit from it.
16. There were only two books named after women in the Bible; they were Esther and Ruth.
17. Methuselah was the oldest person in the Bible; he lived to be 969 years old.
18. Two people who never died in the Bible were Enoch and Elijah.
19. The Levites could not serve in the Tabernacle until they were 25 years old, and they had to retire at the age of 50.
20. David's praise team consisted of over 4,000 men.
21. Noah's ark only had one window.
22. Sarah is the most frequently mentioned woman in the Bible; her name was mentioned 57 times.

23. The Bible was originally written in three languages, Hebrew, Aramaic, and Greek.
24. There are 613 laws in the Torah, and out of this number, 248 are things we should do, and 365 are things we should not do.
25. Adam and Eve were not expelled from the Garden because they sinned; they were expelled from the Garden of Eden to keep them from eating from the Tree of Life.
26. At an average pace, it would take a person seventy hours and forty minutes to read the Bible out loud.
27. Delilah did not cut Samson's hair; her servant did (see Judges 16:19).
28. There were four animals used in the plagues against Egypt; they were: lice, frogs, locusts, and flies.
29. There are at least 185 songs in the Bible.
30. In Acts 20:7-12, the Apostle Paul preached so long that a man named Eutychus fell from the balcony and died. Paul completed his sermon by resurrecting the man.
31. Solomon had 700 wives and 300 concubines.
32. After His resurrection, Jesus lived on Earth for a total of forty days.
33. Noah was 600 years old when he built the ark.
34. The world's largest Bible weighs 1,094 pounds.
35. In the Gospels, Jesus referred to Himself as the "Son of Man" 79 times.
36. The longest name in the Bible is "Mahershalalhashbaz" (Sound it out).
37. There were two men named Lazarus in the Bible. One was a beggar (see Luke 16:19-31) and the other was the man Jesus raised from the dead (see John 11).
38. The youngest king in the Bible was Jehoash at seven-years old.
39. The Bible says that Moses was the meekest man (outside of Jesus) to ever live.
40. Apostle Paul is believed to have written the 14 books of the New Testament.

Thy word is a lamp unto my feet, and a light unto my path.

Psalm 119:105

APOSTASY, HERESY, BLASPHEMY

Apostasy

late 14c., "renunciation, abandonment or neglect of established religion," from Late Latin apostasia, from later Greek apostasia for earlier apostasis "revolt, defection," literally "a standing off," from apostanai "to stand away" (see apostate (n.)). General (non-religious) sense "abandonment of what one has professed" is attested from 1570s.

Source: Bible Study Tools/International Standard Bible Encylopedia

Apostasy

the abandonment or renunciation of a religious or political belief.

Source: Oxford Languages

Greek Word (apostasia)

Definition	Defection	Rebellion	Revolt

In short, apostasy or to be apostate means to reject the gospel of Jesus Christ after having formerly accepted it.

Jude 1:3-4

Beloved, when I gave all diligence to write unto you of the common salvation, it was needful for me to write unto you, and exhort you that ye should earnestly contend for the faith which was once delivered unto the saints. For there are certain men crept in unawares, who were before of old ordained to this condemnation, ungodly men, turning the grace of our God into lasciviousness, and denying the only Lord God, and our Lord Jesus Christ.

Galatians 1:6-9

I marvel that ye are so soon removed from him that called you into the grace of Christ unto another gospel: Which is not another; but there be some that trouble you, and would pervert the gospel of Christ. But though we, or an angel from heaven, preach any other gospel unto you than that which we have preached unto you, let him be accursed. As we said before, so say I now again, If any man preach any other gospel unto you than that ye have received, let him be accursed.

Heresy

From a Greek word signifying (1) a choice, (2) the opinion chosen, and (3) the sect holding the opinion. In the Acts of the Apostles (5:17; 15:5; Isaiah 24:5 Isaiah 24:14; 26:5) it denotes a sect, without reference to its character. Elsewhere, however, in the New Testament it has a different meaning attached to it. Paul ranks "heresies" with crimes and seditions (Galatians 5:20). This word also denotes divisions or schisms in the church (1 Corinthians 11:19). In Titus 3:10 a "heretical person" is one who follows his own self-willed "questions," and who is to be avoided. Heresies thus came to signify self-chosen doctrines not emanating from God (2 Peter 2:1).

Source: Bible Study Tools/International Standard Bible Encyclopedia

Heresy

adherence to a religious opinion contrary to church dogma

Source: Merriam Webster

Greek Word (hairesis)

Definition	Choice	Opinion	Discord

In short, to be a heretic means to express, publish or even promote a religious opinion that goes against what is widely accepted in a specific locale.

2 Peter 2:1-3

But there were false prophets also among the people, even as there shall be false teachers among you, who privily shall bring in damnable heresies, even denying the Lord that bought them, and bring upon themselves swift destruction. And many shall follow their pernicious ways; by reason of whom the way of truth shall be evil spoken of. And through covetousness shall they with feigned words make merchandise of you: whose judgment now of a long time lingereth not, and their damnation slumbereth not.

Titus 3:10-11

A man that is an heretick after the first and second admonition reject; knowing that he that is such is subverted, and sinneth, being condemned of himself.

Blasphemy
In English "blasphemy" denotes any utterance that insults God or Christ (or Allah, or Muhammed) and gives deeply felt offense to their followers. In several states in the United States and in Britain, blasphemy is a criminal offense, although there have been few prosecutions in this century. In Islamic countries generally no distinction is made between blasphemy and heresy, so that any perceived rejection of the Prophet or his message, by Muslims or non-Muslims, is regarded as blasphemous. The biblical concept is very different. There is no Hebrew word equivalent to the English "blasphemy, " and the Greek root *blasphem-* [blasfhmevw], which is used fifty-five times in the New Testament, has a wide meaning. In both Testaments the idea of blasphemy as something that offends the religious sensibilities of others is completely absent.
Source: Bible Study Tools/International Standard Bible Encyclopedia

Blasphemy
the act or offense of speaking sacrilegiously about God or sacred things; profane talk.
Source: Oxford Languages

Greek Word (blasphémia)			
Definition	Slander	Abusive Language	Railing Accusation

In short, the word "blasphemy" means to call that which is good "evil," and to call that which is evil "good." It means to exchange the truth of God for a lie.

Matthew 12:31-32
Wherefore I say unto you, All manner of sin and blasphemy shall be forgiven unto men: but the blasphemy against the Holy Ghost shall not be forgiven unto men. And whosoever speaketh a word against the Son of man, it shall be forgiven him: but whosoever speaketh against the Holy Ghost, it shall not be forgiven him, neither in this world, neither in the world to come.

Seven Churches in Revelations

Church	Brief Overview
Ephesus	The church that wandered away from her first love.
Smyrna	The church that remains faithful in the face of persecution.
Pergamos	The heretic/apostate church.
Thyatira	The church that tolerates false apostles.
Sardis	The spiritually dead church.
Philadelphia	The church that, amidst its weaknesses, endures trials.
Laodicea	The lukewarm church.

Ephesus
Revelation 2:1-7

"To the angel of the church in Ephesus write: These are the words of him who holds the seven stars in his right hand and walks among the seven golden lampstands. I know your deeds, your hard work and your perseverance. I know that you cannot tolerate wicked people, that you have tested those who claim to be apostles but are not, and have found them false. You have persevered and have endured hardships for my name, and have not grown weary. Yet I hold this against you: You have forsaken the love you had at first. Consider how far you have fallen! Repent and do the things you did at first. If you do not repent, I will come to you and remove your lampstand from its place. But you have this in your favor: You hate the practices of the Nicolaitans, which I also hate. Whoever has ears, let them hear what the Spirit says to the churches. To the one who is victorious, I will give the right to eat from the tree of life, which is in the paradise of God.

Smyrna
Revelation 2:8-11

"To the angel of the church in Smyrna write: These are the words of him who is the First and the Last, who died and came to life again. I know your afflictions and your poverty-yet you are rich! I know about the slander of those who say they are Jews and are not, but are a synagogue of Satan. Do not be afraid of what you are about to suffer. I tell you, the devil will put some of you in prison to test you, and you will suffer persecution for ten days. Be faithful, even to the point of death, and I will give you life as your victor's crown. Whoever has ears, let them hear what the Spirit says to the churches. The one who is victorious will not be hurt at all by the second death.

Pergamos
Revelation 2:12-17

"To the angel of the church in Pergamum write: These are the words of him who has the sharp, double-edged sword. I know where you live-where Satan has his throne. Yet you remain true to my name. You did not renounce your faith in me, not even in the days of Antipas, my faithful witness, who was put to death in your city-where Satan lives. Nevertheless, I have a few things against you: There are some among you who hold to the teaching of Balaam, who taught Balak to entice the Israelites to sin so that they ate food sacrificed to idols and committed sexual immorality. Likewise, you also have those who hold to the teaching of the Nicolaitans. Repent therefore! Otherwise, I will soon come to you and will fight against them with the sword of my mouth. Whoever has ears, let them hear what the Spirit says to the churches. To the one who is victorious, I will give some of the hidden manna. I will also give that person a white stone with a new name written on it, known only to the one who receives it.

Thyatira
Revelation 2:18-29

"To the angel of the church in Thyatira write: These are the words of the Son of God, whose eyes are like blazing fire and whose feet are like burnished bronze. I know your deeds, your love and faith, your service and perseverance, and that you are now doing more than you did at first. Nevertheless, I have this against you: You tolerate that woman Jezebel, who calls herself a prophet. By her teaching she misleads my servants into sexual immorality and the eating of food sacrificed to idols. I have given her time to repent of her immorality, but she is unwilling. So I will cast her on a bed of suffering, and I will make those who commit adultery with her suffer intensely, unless they repent of her ways. I will strike her children dead. Then all the churches will know that I am he who searches hearts and minds, and I will repay each of you according to your deeds. Now I say to the rest of you in Thyatira, to you who do not hold to her teaching and have not learned Satan's so-called deep secrets, 'I will not impose any other burden on you, except to hold on to what you have until I come.' To the one who is victorious and does my will to the end, I will give authority over the nations- that one 'will rule them with an iron scepter and will dash them to pieces like pottery'-just as I have received authority from my Father. I will also give that one the morning star. Whoever has ears, let them hear what the Spirit says to the churches.

Sardis

Revelation 3:1-6

"To the angel of the church in Sardis write: These are the words of him who holds the seven spirits of God and the seven stars. I know your deeds; you have a reputation of being alive, but you are dead. Wake up! Strengthen what remains and is about to die, for I have found your deeds unfinished in the sight of my God. Remember, therefore, what you have received and heard; hold it fast, and repent. But if you do not wake up, I will come like a thief, and you will not know at what time I will come to you. Yet you have a few people in Sardis who have not soiled their clothes. They will walk with me, dressed in white, for they are worthy. The one who is victorious will, like them, be dressed in white. I will never blot out the name of that person from the book of life, but will acknowledge that name before my Father and his angels. Whoever has ears, let them hear what the Spirit says to the churches.

Philadelphia

Revelation 3:7-13

"To the angel of the church in Philadelphia write: These are the words of him who is holy and true, who holds the key of David. What he opens no one can shut, and what he shuts no one can open. I know your deeds. See, I have placed before you an open door that no one can shut. I know that you have little strength, yet you have kept my word and have not denied my name. I will make those who are of the synagogue of Satan, who claim to be Jews though they are not, but are liars—I will make them come and fall down at your feet and acknowledge that I have loved you. Since you have kept my command to endure patiently, I will also keep you from the hour of trial that is going to come on the whole world to test the inhabitants of the earth. I am coming soon. Hold on to what you have, so that no one will take your crown. The one who is victorious I will make a pillar in the temple of my God. Never again will they leave it. I will write on them the name of my God and the name of the city of my God, the new Jerusalem, which is coming down out of heaven from my God; and I will also write on them my new name. Whoever has ears, let them hear what the Spirit says to the churches.

Laodicea

Revelation 3:14-22

"To the angel of the church in Laodicea write: These are the words of the Amen, the faithful and true witness, the ruler of God's creation. I know your deeds, that you are neither cold nor hot. I wish you were either one or the other! So, because you are lukewarm—neither hot nor cold—I am about to spit you out of my mouth. You say, 'I am rich; I have acquired wealth and do not need a thing.' But you do not realize that you are wretched, pitiful, poor, blind and naked. I counsel you to buy from me gold refined in the fire, so you can become rich; and white clothes to wear, so you can cover your shameful nakedness; and salve to put on your eyes, so you can see. Those whom I love I rebuke and discipline. So be earnest and repent. Here I am! I stand at the door and knock. If anyone hears my voice and opens the door, I will come in and eat with that person, and they with me. To the one who is victorious, I will give the right to sit with me on my throne, just as I was victorious and sat down with my Father on his throne. Whoever has ears, let them hear what the Spirit says to the churches."

Biblical Significance of the Number Seven

Used 735 times (54 times in the book of Revelation alone), the number 7 is the foundation of God's Word. If we include with this count how many times 'sevenfold' (6) and 'seventh' (119) is used, our total jumps to 860 references.

Seven is the number of completeness and perfection (both physical and spiritual). It derives much of its meaning from being tied directly to God's creation of all things. According to some Jewish traditions, the creation of Adam occurred on September 26, 3760 B.C. (or the first day of Tishri, which is the seventh month on the Hebrew calendar). The word 'created' is used 7 times describing God's creative work (Genesis 1:1, 21, 27 three times; 2:3; 2:4). There are 7 days in a week and God's Sabbath is on the 7th day.

The Bible, as a whole, was originally divided into 7 major divisions. They are 1) the Law; 2) the Prophets; 3) the Writings, or Psalms; 4) the Gospels and Acts; 5) the General Epistles; 6) the Epistles of Paul; and 7) the book of Revelation. The total number of originally inspired books was forty-nine, or 7 x 7, demonstrating the absolute perfection of the Word of God.

Source: BibleStudy.org

Test Your Knowledge

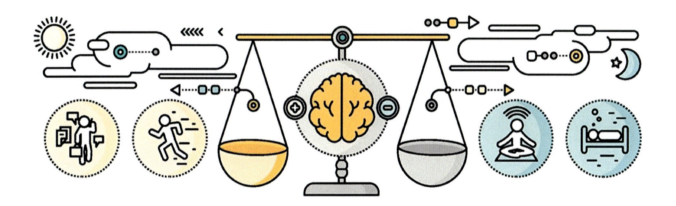

Test Your Knowledge

BOOKS OF THE BIBLE (EXAM)

Using the slots below, list the 66 books of the Bible. Try to list them in the correct order. Note, you can use the color chart to help you remember the books.

167

Test Your Knowledge

Bible Facts (Activity)

List 12 Bible facts you learned from this book.

1	
2	
3	
4	
5	
6	
7	
8	
9	
10	
11	
12	

Test Your Knowledge

Questions and Answers

What is the SOAP Method?

Your Answer

What is Bible Journaling?

Your Answer

Test Your Knowledge

What is the difference between Gehenna, the Abyss, Hell, and the Lake of Fire?

Your Answer

List 5 signs you are in a cult.

	Your Answer
1	
2	
3	
4	
5	

Test Your Knowledge

List 5 facts about angels.

	Your Answer
1	
2	
3	
4	
5	

List 5 facts about demons.

	Your Answer
1	
2	
3	
4	
5	

Bible Symbols (Exam)

What does the following Bible symbols mean?	
Symbol	Meaning
The Rainbow	
Stairway	
Thunder, Lightning, Cloud and Smoke	
Thunder	
Trumpets	
Pillar of Cloud and Fire	
Throne	
Dry Bones	
White Hair	
Wind	
Fire	
Stars and Lampstands	
Signet Ring	
Arrows	
Sceptre	
Capstone	
Rock	
Human Body	
Grass	

Test Your Knowledge

Seven Churches (Exam)

What are the seven churches in Revelations, and what do they represent? After you've answered the question, do some extensive research on each of the churches, making sure to list where they were located and what was significant about each church.

Church	Represent

Made in the USA
Middletown, DE
27 April 2021